HUMAN CAPITAL
A Theoretical and Empirical Analysis, with Special Reference to Education

National Bureau of Economic Research
Number 80, General Series

Human Capital

A THEORETICAL AND EMPIRICAL ANALYSIS, WITH SPECIAL REFERENCE TO EDUCATION

BY

GARY S. BECKER

Columbia University

PUBLISHED BY

NATIONAL BUREAU OF ECONOMIC RESEARCH

NEW YORK

Distributed by
Columbia University Press
New York and London
1964

Printed in the United States of America

Relation of the Directors to the Work and Publications
of the National Bureau of Economic Research

1. The object of the National Bureau of Economic Research is to ascertain and to present to the public important economic facts and their interpretation in a scientific and impartial manner. The Board of Directors is charged with the responsibility of ensuring that the work of the National Bureau is carried on in strict conformity with this object.

2. To this end the Board of Directors shall appoint one or more Directors of Research.

3. The Director or Directors of Research shall submit to the members of the Board, or to its Executive Committee, for their formal adoption, all specific proposals concerning researches to be instituted.

4. No report shall be published until the Director or Directors of Research shall have submitted to the Board a summary drawing attention to the character of the data and their utilization in the report, the nature and treatment of the problems involved, the main conclusions, and such other information as in their opinion would serve to determine the suitability of the report for publication in accordance with the principles of the National Bureau.

5. A copy of any manuscript proposed for publication shall also be submitted to each member of the Board. For each manuscript to be so submitted a special committee shall be appointed by the President, or at his designation by the Executive Director, consisting of three Directors selected as nearly as may be one from each general division of the Board. The names of the special manuscript committee shall be stated to each Director when the summary and report described in paragraph (4) are sent to him. It shall be the duty of each member of the committee to read the manuscript. If each member of the special committee signifies his approval within thirty days, the manuscript may be published. If each member of the special committee has not signified his approval within thirty days of the transmittal of the report and manuscript, the Director of Research shall then notify each member of the Board, requesting approval or disapproval of publication, and thirty additional days shall be granted for this purpose. The manuscript shall then not be published unless at least a majority of the entire Board and a two-thirds majority of those members of the Board who shall have voted on the proposal within the time fixed for the receipt of votes on the publication proposed shall have approved.

6. No manuscript may be published, though approved by each member of the special committee, until forty-five days have elapsed from the transmittal of the summary and report. The interval is allowed for the receipt of any memorandum of dissent or reservation, together with a brief statement of his reasons, that any member may wish to express; and such memorandum of dissent or reservation shall be published with the manuscript if he so desires. Publication does not, however, imply that each member of the Board has read the manuscript, or that either members of the Board in general, or of the special committee, have passed upon its validity in every detail.

7. A copy of this resolution shall, unless otherwise determined by the Board, be printed in each copy of every National Bureau book.

(Resolution adopted October 25, 1926, as revised February 6, 1933, and February 24, 1941)

vi

To my wife Doria

*For encouragement and support during
a long period of production*

This study was made possible by funds granted by the Carnegie Corporation of New York to the National Bureau. The Carnegie Corporation is, however, not to be understood as approving or disapproving by virtue of its grant any of the statements made or views expressed herein.

Contents

ix

Contents

Appendixes

Tables

Tables

Tables

Charts

Preface

THE origin of this study can be traced both to the finding that a substantial growth in income in the United States remains after the growth in physical capital and labor has been accounted for and to the emphasis of some economists on the importance of education in promoting economic development. My original intention was to shed some exploratory light on these issues by bringing together readily available information from Census reports on the incomes of persons with different amounts of education and from the Office of Education on the costs of education. For if education were economically important, I reasoned, money rates of return on education ought to be significant.

A long time has elapsed between the start, back in 1957, and the appearance of this monograph presenting the full analysis. During that time interest in the economics of education has mushroomed throughout the world and stimulated a profusion of research and policy proposals. Estimates have been made of the amounts invested in and the rates of return on education in both rich and poor countries. Perhaps some of the expanding interest can be traced to preliminary reports on the National Bureau study.[1]

This interest and further reflection, in turn, encouraged me to transform the original aim into a more ambitious undertaking. I became interested in the general theory of investment in human capital with its ramifications for a variety of economic phenomena. The theoretical analysis in turn led to an empirical examination of several other effects of education, such as those centering around the shapes

[1] The previously published reports consist of "Underinvestment in College Education?" *American Economic Review,* May 1960, and "Investment in Human Capital: A Theoretical Analysis," *Investment in Human Beings,* NBER Special Conference 15, supplement to *Journal of Political Economy,* October 1962.

xv

of age-earnings and age-wealth profiles. Finally, the discussion of rates of return covers a wider variety of evidence, groups, time periods, and implications than in other studies.

Support, assistance, and criticism were generously provided by many institutions and persons during the course of this study. Let me first thank the Carnegie Corporation of New York for their two grants to the National Bureau to explore work on the economic effects of education. Leave from teaching duties was provided by the Ford Professorship at Columbia University during the academic year 1960–61, and a Ford Faculty Fellowship during 1963–64.

The study would have been impossible without the aid of a series of unusually able and conscientious research assistants. Major contributions were made by Rosanne Cole, Linda Kee, and Eugenia Scandrett, with additional assistance from Mary Holman Faden, Shirley Johnson, and June Cohn.

T. W. Schultz, the major figure in the economics of education, has been liberal with encouragement and most helpful with criticism. I feel greatly indebted to him, and would like to record my appreciation here. Jacob Mincer has been exceedingly helpful in countless discussions and on numerous drafts with suggestions, criticisms, and that intangible asset—enthusiasm.

The National Bureau reading committee played an important role in improving the content. I am indebted to George J. Stigler, Richard Easterlin, Albert Fishlow, Milton Friedman, and Zvi Griliches. Many others commented on all or parts of various drafts. I would like to acknowledge the helpful contributions of M. Blaug, Arthur F. Burns, Edward F. Denison, Evsey Domar, Solomon Fabricant, Victor R. Fuchs, Leo Goodman, W. Lee Hansen, Hendrick Houthakker, C. Harry Kahn, James N. Morgan, Selma Mushkin, Alice Rivlin, and of various participants in the Labor Workshop at Columbia University. Members of the National Bureau Board of Directors who provided useful comments were V. W. Bladen, Marion B. Folsom, W. Allen Wallis, and Joseph H. Willits.

I am grateful to the editorial staff of the National Bureau, especially to Marie-Christine Culbert for her detailed and incisive comments. H. Irving Forman skillfully drew the charts.

CHAPTER I

Introduction

SOME activities primarily affect future well-being; the main impact of others is in the present. Some affect money income and others psychic income, that is, consumption. Sailing primarily affects consumption, on-the-job training primarily affects money income, and a college education could affect both. These effects may operate either through physical resources or through human resources. This study is concerned with activities that influence future monetary and psychic income by increasing the resources in people. These activities are called investments in human capital.

The many forms of such investments include schooling, on-the-job training, medical care, migration, and searching for information about prices and incomes. They differ in their effects on earnings and consumption, in the amounts typically invested, in the size of returns, and in the extent to which the connection between investment and return is perceived. But all these investments improve skills, knowledge, or health, and thereby raise money or psychic incomes.

Recent years have witnessed intensive concern with and research on investment in human capital, much of it contributed or stimulated by T. W. Schultz. The main motivating factor has probably been a realization that the growth of physical capital, at least as conventionally measured, explains a relatively small part of the growth of income in most countries. The search for better explanations has led to improved measures of physical capital and to an interest in less tangible entities, such as technological change and human capital. Also behind this concern is the strong dependence of modern military technology on education and skills, the rapid growth in expenditures on education and health, the age-old quest for an understanding of the personal distribution of income, the

1

recent growth in unemployment in the United States, the Leontief scarce-factor paradox, and several other important economic problems.

The result has been the accumulation of a tremendous amount of circumstantial evidence testifying to the economic importance of human capital, especially of education. Probably the most impressive piece of evidence is that more highly educated and skilled persons almost always tend to earn more than others. This is true of developed countries as different as the United States and the Soviet Union, of underdeveloped countries as different as India and Cuba, and of the United States one hundred years ago as well as today. Moreover, few, if any, countries have achieved a sustained period of economic development without having invested substantial amounts in their labor force, and most studies that have attempted quantitative assessments of contributions to growth have assigned an important role to investment in human capital. Again, inequality in the distribution of earnings and income is generally positively related to inequality in education and other training. To take a final example, unemployment tends to be strongly related, usually inversely, to education.

Passions are easily aroused on this subject and even people who are generally in favor of education, medical care, and the like often dislike the phrase "human capital" and still more any emphasis on its economic effects. They are often the people who launch the most bitter attacks on research on human capital, partly because they fear that emphasis on the "material" effects of human capital detracts from its "cultural" effects, which to them are more important. Those denying the economic importance of education and other investments in human capital have attacked the circumstantial evidence in its favor. They argue that the correlation between earnings and investment in human capital is due to a correlation between ability and investment in human capital, or to the singling out of the most favorable groups, such as white male college graduates, and to the consequent neglect of women, drop-outs, nonwhites, or high-school graduates. They consider the true correlation to be very weak, and, therefore, a poor guide and of little help to people investing in human capital. The association between education and economic development or between inequality in education and income is attributed to the effect of income on education, considering education as a consumption good, and hence of no greater causal significance than the association between automobile ownership and economic development or between the inequality in ownership and incomes.

Introduction

This study hopes to contribute to knowledge in this area by going far beyond circumstantial evidence and analysis. Part One treats the theory of investment in human capital in detail and reveals its importance through the wide variety of economic phenomena that it encompasses. Chapter II derives a number of important effects of such investments on earnings and employment, while Chapter III shows how to estimate the total amount invested and how it changes when the anticipated gains change.

Part Two presents various empirical tests of the theoretical analysis. Chapters IV and V estimate the gains from college education in the United States in recent years. Costs as well as returns are considered, and estimates are presented not only for selected groups, such as white male college graduates, but also for typical college entrants (sections 1 and 3 of Chapter IV). Detailed attention is paid to the effect of the correlation between education and ability, and to the variation in the gain from college (sections 2 and 4 of Chapter IV). Social as well as private gains are estimated, and both are compared to corresponding estimates for physical capital (Chapter V).

Chapter VI briefly extends the discussion to high-school education, considering social as well as private costs and returns, and the effect of differential ability (section 1). This chapter also tries to discover the secular trend in the United States during the twentieth century in the economic effects of high-school and college education (section 2).

Chapter VII tests the implications of the theoretical analysis concerning the effect of human capital on the shape of age-earnings profiles (section 1). Also considered is the effect on the relation between age and the discounted value of subsequent earnings, which are called age-wealth profiles. These profiles are applied to the study of life-cycle variations in savings and consumption, and in a few other ways (section 2).

Perhaps it is best to conclude the introduction by emphasizing that the attention paid to the economic effects of education and other human capital in this study is not in any way meant to imply that other effects are unimportant, or less important than the economic ones. The advantages of a division of labor are no less real here than they are in research in general. I would like to urge simply that the economic effects are important and they have been relatively neglected, at least until recently.

3

PART ONE
THEORETICAL ANALYSIS

"The most valuable of all capital is
that invested in human beings."

Alfred Marshall, *Principles of Economics*

CHAPTER II

Investment in Human Capital: Effects on Earnings[1]

THE original aim of this study was to estimate the money rate of return to college and high-school education in the United States. In order to set these estimates in the proper context, a brief formulation of the theory of investment in human capital was undertaken. It soon became clear to me, however, that more than a restatement was called for; while important and pioneering work had been done on the economic return to various occupations and education classes,[2] there had been few, if any, attempts to treat the process of investing in people from a general viewpoint or to work out a broad set of empirical implications. I began then to prepare a general analysis of investment in human capital.

It eventually became apparent that this general analysis would do much more than fill a gap in formal economic theory: it offers a unified explanation of a wide range of empirical phenomena which have either been given *ad hoc* interpretations or have baffled investigators. Among these phenomena are the following: (1) Earnings typically increase with age at a decreasing rate. Both the rate of increase and

---

[1] This chapter and the one that follows were published in somewhat different form in *Investment in Human Beings,* NBER Special Conference 15, supplement to *Journal of Political Economy,* October 1962, pp. 9-49.

[2] In addition to the earlier works of Smith, Mill, and Marshall, see the brilliant work (which greatly influenced my own thinking about occupational choice) by M. Friedman and S. Kuznets, *Income from Independent Professional Practice,* New York, NBER, 1945; see also H. Clark, *Life Earnings in Selected Occupations in the U.S.,* New York, 1937; J. R. Walsh, "Capital Concept Applied to Man," *Quarterly Journal of Economics,* February 1935; G. Stigler and D. Blank, *The Demand and Supply of Scientific Personnel,* New York, NBER, 1957. In recent years, of course, there has been considerable work, especially by T. W. Schultz; see, for example, his "Investment in Human Capital," *American Economic Review,* March 1961, pp. 1-17.

the rate of retardation tend to be positively related to the level of skill. (2) Unemployment rates tend to be inversely related to the level of skill. (3) Firms in underdeveloped countries appear to be more "paternalistic" toward employees than those in developed countries. (4) Younger persons change jobs more frequently and receive more schooling and on-the-job training than older persons do. (5) The distribution of earnings is positively skewed, especially among professional and other skilled workers. (6) Abler persons receive more education and other kinds of training than others. (7) The division of labor is limited by the extent of the market. (8) The typical investor in human capital is more impetuous and thus more likely to err than is the typical investor in tangible capital.

What a diverse and even confusing array! Yet all these, as well as many other important empirical implications, can be derived from very simple theoretical arguments. The purpose here is to set out these arguments in general form, with the emphasis placed on empirical implications, although little empirical material is presented. Systematic empirical work appears in Part Two.

In this chapter a lengthy discussion of on-the-job training is presented and then, much more briefly, discussions of investment in schooling, information, and health. On-the-job training is dealt with so elaborately not because it is more important than other kinds of investment in human capital—although its importance is often underrated—but because it clearly illustrates the effect of human capital on earnings, employment, and other economic variables. For example, the close connection between indirect and direct costs and the effect of human capital on earnings at different ages are vividly brought out. The extended discussion of on-the-job training paves the way for much briefer discussions of other kinds of investment in human beings.

1. On-the-Job Training

Theories of firm behavior, no matter how they differ in other respects, almost invariably ignore the effect of the productive process itself on worker productivity. This is not to say that no one recognizes that productivity is affected by the job itself; but the recognition has not been formalized, incorporated into economic analysis, and its implications worked out. I now intend to do just that, placing special emphasis on the broader economic implications.

Many workers increase their productivity by learning new skills and perfecting old ones while on the job. Presumably, future productivity can be improved only at a cost, for otherwise there would be an unlimited demand for training. Included in cost are the value placed on the time and effort of trainees, the "teaching" provided by others, and the equipment and materials used. These are costs in the sense that they could have been used in producing current output if they had not been used in raising future output. The amount spent and the duration of the training period depend partly on the type of training since more is spent for a longer time on, say, an intern than a machine operator.

Consider explicitly now a firm that is hiring employees for a specified time period (in the limiting case this period approaches zero), and for the moment assume that both labor and product markets are perfectly competitive. If there were no on-the-job training, wage rates would be given to the firm and would be independent of its actions. A profit-maximizing firm would be in equilibrium when marginal products equaled wages, that is, when marginal receipts equaled marginal expenditures. In symbols

$$MP = W, \tag{1}$$

where W equals wages or expenditures and MP equals the marginal product or receipts. Firms would not worry too much about the relation between labor conditions in the present and future, partly because workers would only be hired for one period and partly because wages and marginal products in future periods would be independent of a firm's current behavior. It can therefore legitimately be assumed that workers have unique marginal products (for given amounts of other inputs) and wages in each period, which are, respectively, the maximum productivity in all possible uses and the market wage rate. A more complete set of equilibrium conditions would be the set

$$MP_t = W_t, \tag{2}$$

where t refers to the tth period. The equilibrium position for each period would depend only on the flows during that period.

These conditions are altered when account is taken of on-the-job training and the connection thereby created between present and future receipts and expenditures. Training might lower current re-

9

ceipts and raise current expenditures, yet firms could profitably provide this training if future receipts were sufficiently raised or future expenditures sufficiently lowered. Expenditures during each period need not equal wages, receipts need not equal the maximum possible marginal productivity, and expenditures and receipts during all periods would be interrelated. The set of equilibrium conditions summarized in equation (2) would be replaced by an equality between the *present values* of receipts and expenditures. If E_t and R_t represent expenditures and receipts during period t, and i the market discount rate, then the equilibrium condition can be written as

$$\sum_{t=0}^{n-1} \frac{R_t}{(1+i)^{t+1}} = \sum_{t=0}^{n-1} \frac{E_t}{(1+i)^{t+1}}, \tag{3}$$

when n represents the number of periods, and R_t and E_t depend on all other receipts and expenditures. The equilibrium condition of equation (2) has been generalized, for if marginal product equals wages in each period, the present value of the marginal product stream would have to equal the present value of the wage stream. Obviously, however, the converse need not hold.

If training were given only during the initial period, expenditures during the initial period would equal wages plus the outlay on training, expenditures during other periods would equal wages alone, and receipts during all periods would equal marginal products. Equation (3) becomes

$$MP_0 + \sum_{t=1}^{n-1} \frac{MP_t}{(1+i)^t} = W_0 + k + \sum_{t=1}^{n-1} \frac{W_t}{(1+i)^t}, \tag{4}$$

where k measures the outlay on training.

If a new term is defined,

$$G = \sum_{t=1}^{n-1} \frac{MP_t - W_t}{(1+i)^t}, \tag{5}$$

equation (4) can be written as

$$MP_0 + G = W_0 + k. \tag{6}$$

Since the term k only measures the actual outlay on training, it does not entirely measure training costs, for it excludes the time that a person spends on this training, time that could have been used to produce current output. The difference between what could have been produced, MP_0', and what is produced, MP_0, is the opportunity cost of the time spent in training. If C is defined as the sum of opportunity costs and outlays on training, (6) becomes

$$MP_0' + G = W_0 + C. \tag{7}$$

The term G, the excess of future receipts over future outlays, is a measure of the return to the firm from providing training; and, therefore, the difference between G and C measures the difference between the return from and the cost of training. Equation (7) shows that the marginal product would equal wages in the initial period only when the return equals costs, or G equals C; it would be greater or less than wages as the return was smaller or greater than costs. Those familiar with capital theory might argue that this generalization of the simple equality between marginal product and wages is spurious because a full equilibrium would require equality between the return from an investment—in this case, made on the job—and costs. If this implied that G equals C, marginal product would equal wages in the initial period. There is much to be said for the relevance of a condition equating the return from an investment with costs, but such a condition does not imply that G equals C or that marginal product equals wages. The following discussion demonstrates that great care is required in the application of this condition to on-the-job investment.

Our treatment of on-the-job training produced some general results —summarized in equations (3) and (7)—of wide applicability, but more concrete results require more specific assumptions. In the following sections two types of on-the-job training are discussed in turn: general and specific.

GENERAL TRAINING

General training is useful in many firms besides those providing it; for example, a machinist trained in the army finds his skills of value in steel and aircraft firms, and a doctor trained (interned) at one hospital finds his skills useful at other hospitals. Most on-the-job training presumably increases the future marginal productivity of workers in the firms providing it; general training, however, also increases their marginal product in many other firms as well. Since in a competitive labor market the wage rates paid by any firm are determined by marginal productivities in other firms, future wage rates as well as marginal products would increase in firms providing general training. These firms could capture some of the return from training only if their marginal product rose by more than their wages. "Perfectly general" training would be equally useful in many firms and marginal products would rise by the same extent in all of them. Consequently, wage rates would rise by exactly the same amount as the marginal product and the firms providing such training could not capture any of the return.

Why, then, would rational firms in competitive labor markets provide general training if it did not bring any return? The answer is that firms would provide general training only if they did not have to pay any of the costs. Persons receiving general training would be willing to pay these costs since training raises their future wages. Hence it is the trainees, not the firms, who would bear the cost of general training and profit from the return.[3]

These and other implications of general training can be more formally demonstrated in equation (7). Since wages and marginal products are raised by the same amount, MP_t must equal W_t for all $t = 1, \ldots n - 1$, and therefore

$$G = \sum_{t=1}^{n-1} \frac{MP_t - W_t}{(1 + i)^t} = 0. \tag{8}$$

Equation (7) is reduced to

$$MP_0' = W_0 + C, \tag{9}$$

or

$$W_0 = MP_0' - C. \tag{10}$$

[3] Some persons have asked why any general training is provided if firms do not collect any of the returns. The answer is simply that they have an incentive to do so wherever the demand price for training is at least as great as the supply price or cost of providing the training. Workers in turn would prefer to be trained on the job rather than in specialized firms (schools) if the training and work complemented each other (see the discussion in section 2 below).

In terms of actual marginal product

$$MP_0 = W_0 + k, \qquad (9')$$

or

$$W_0 = MP_0 - k. \qquad (10')$$

The wage of trainees would not equal their opportunity marginal product but would be less by the total cost of training. In other words, employees would pay for general training by receiving wages below their current (opportunity) productivity. Equation (10) has many other implications, and the rest of this section is devoted to developing the more important ones.

Some might argue that a really "net" definition of marginal product, obtained by subtracting training costs from "gross" marginal product, must equal wages even for trainees. Such an interpretation of net productivity could formally save the equality between marginal product and wages here, but not always, as shown later. Moreover, regardless of which interpretation is used, training costs would have to be included in any study of the relation between wages and productivity.

Employees pay for general on-the-job training by receiving wages below what they could receive elsewhere. "Earnings" during the training period would be the difference between an income or flow term (potential marginal product) and a capital or stock term (training costs), so that the capital and income accounts would be closely intermixed, with changes in either affecting wages. In other words, earnings of persons receiving on-the-job training would be net of investment costs and would correspond to the definition of *net* earnings used throughout this paper, which subtracts all investment costs from "gross" earnings. Therefore, our departure with this definition of earnings from the accounting conventions used for transactions in material goods—which separate income from capital accounts to prevent a transaction in capital from *ipso facto*[4] affecting the income side—is not capricious but is grounded in a fundamental difference between the way investment in material and human capital are "written off." The underlying cause of this difference undoubtedly is the widespread reluctance to treat people as capital and the accompanying tendency to treat all wage receipts as earnings.

---

[4] Of course, a shift between assets with different productivities would affect the income account on material goods even with current accounting practices.

Intermixing the capital and income accounts could make the reported "incomes" of trainees unusually low and perhaps negative, even though their long-run or lifetime incomes were well above average. Since a considerable fraction of young persons receive some training, and since trainees tend to have lower current and higher subsequent earnings than other youth, the correlation of current consumption with the current earnings of young males[5] would not only be much weaker than the correlation with long-run earnings, but the signs of these correlations might even differ.[6]

Doubt has been cast on the frequent assertion that no allowance is made in the income accounts for depreciation on human capital.[7] A depreciation-type item is deducted, at least from the earnings due to on-the-job training, for the cost would be deducted during the training period. Depreciation on tangible capital does not bulk so large in any one period because it is usually "written off" or depreciated during a period of time designed to approximate its economic life. Hence human and tangible capital appear to differ more in the time pattern of depreciation than in its existence,[8] and the effect on wage income of a rapid "write-off" of human capital is what should be emphasized and studied.

This point can be demonstrated differently and more rigorously. The ideal depreciation on a capital asset during any period would equal its change in value during the period. In particular, if value

[5] The term "young males" rather than "young families" is used because as J. Mincer has shown (in his "Labor Force Participation of Married Women," *Aspects of Labor Economics,* Princeton for NBER, 1962), the labor force participation of wives is positively correlated with the difference between a husband's long-run and current income. Participation of wives, therefore, makes the correlation between a family's current and a husband's long-run income greater than that between a husband's current and long-run income.

[6] A difference in signs is impossible in Friedman's analysis of consumer behavior because he assumes that, at least in the aggregate, transitory and long-run (that is, permanent) incomes are uncorrelated (see his *A Theory of the Consumption Function,* Princeton for NBER, 1957); I am suggesting that they may be *negatively* correlated for young persons.

[7] See C. Christ, "Patinkin on Money, Interest, and Prices," *Journal of Political Economy,* August 1957, p. 352; and W. Hamburger, "The Relation of Consumption to Wealth and the Wage Rate," *Econometrica,* January 1955.

[8] In a recent paper, R. Goode has argued (see his "Educational Expenditures and the Income Tax," in Selma J. Mushkin, ed., *Economics of Higher Education,* Washington, 1962) that educated persons should be permitted to subtract from income a depreciation allowance on tuition payments. Such an allowance is apparently not required for on-the-job training costs or, as seen later, for the indirect costs of education; indeed, one might argue, on the contrary, that too much or too rapid depreciation is permitted on such investments.

CHART 1

Relation of Earnings to Age

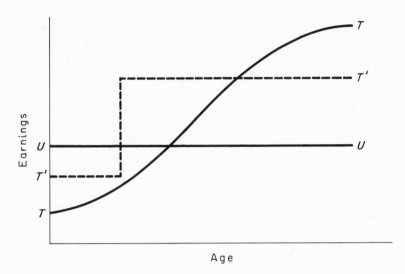

rose, a negative depreciation term would have to be subtracted or a positive appreciation term added to the income from the asset. Since training costs would be deducted from earnings during the training period, the economic "value" of a trainee would at first increase rather than decrease with age, and only later begin to decrease. Therefore, a negative rather than a positive depreciation term would have to be subtracted initially.[9] _

Training has an important effect on the relation between earnings and age. Suppose that untrained persons received the same earnings regardless of age, as shown by the horizontal line *UU* in Chart 1. Trained persons would receive lower earnings during the training period because training is paid for at that time, and higher earnings at later ages because the return is collected then. The combined effect of paying for and collecting the return from training in this way would be to make the age earnings curve of trained persons, shown by *TT* in Chart 1, steeper than that of untrained persons, the difference being greater the greater the cost of, and return from, the investment.

[9] See Chapter VII, section 2, for some empirical estimates of "depreciation" on human capital.

Not only does training make the curve steeper but, as indicated by Chart 1, also more concave; that is, the rate of increase in earnings is affected more at younger than at older ages. Suppose, to take an extreme case, that training raised the level of marginal productivity but had no effect on the slope, so that the marginal productivity of trained persons was also independent of age. If earnings equaled marginal product, TT would merely be parallel to and higher than UU, showing neither slope nor concavity. Since, however, earnings of trained persons would be below marginal productivity during the training period and equal afterward, they would rise sharply at the end of the training period and then level off (as shown by the dashed line $T'T'$ in Chart 1), imparting a concave appearance to the curve as a whole. In this extreme case an extreme concavity appears (as in TT); in less extreme cases the principle would be the same and the concavity more continuous.

Foregone earnings are an important, although neglected, cost of much investment in human capital and should be treated in the same way as direct outlays. Indeed, *all* costs appear as foregone earnings to workers receiving on-the-job training; that is, all costs appear as lower earnings than could be received elsewhere, although direct outlays, C, may really be an important part of costs. The arbitrariness of the division between indirect and direct costs and the resulting advantage of treating total costs as a whole[10] can be further demonstrated by contrasting school and on-the-job training. Usually only the direct costs of school training are emphasized, even though opportunity costs are sometimes (as with college education) an important part of the total. A shift from school training to on-the-job training would, however, reverse the emphasis and make all costs appear as foregone earnings, even when direct outlays were important.

Income-maximizing firms in competitive labor markets would not pay the cost of general training and would pay trained persons the market wage. If, however, training costs were paid, many persons would seek training, few would quit during the training period, and labor costs would be relatively high. Firms that did not pay trained persons the market wage would have difficulty satisfying their skill

[10] The equivalence between indirect and direct costs applies to consumption as well as to investment decisions. In my paper, *A Theory of the Allocation of Time,* IBM Research Paper RC 1149, March 20, 1964, an analysis incorporating both direct and indirect consumption costs is applied to the choice between work and nonwork, price and income elasticities of demand for goods, the economic function of queues, and several other areas.

requirements and would also tend to be less profitable than other firms. Firms that paid both for training and less than the market wage for trained persons would have the worst of both worlds, for they would attract too many trainees and too few trained persons.

These principles have been clearly demonstrated during the last few years in discussions of problems in recruiting military personnel. The military offers training in a wide variety of skills and many are very useful in the civilian sector. Training is provided during part or all of the first enlistment period and used during the remainder of the first period and hopefully during subsequent periods. This hope, however, is thwarted by the fact that re-enlistment rates tend to be inversely related to the amount of civilian-type skills provided by the military.[11] Persons with these skills leave the military more readily because they can receive much higher wages in the civilian sector. Net military wages for those receiving training are higher relative to civilian wages during the first than during subsequent enlistment periods because training costs are largely paid by the military. Not surprisingly, therefore, first-term enlistments for skilled jobs are obtained much more easily than are re-enlistments.

The military is a conspicuous example of an organization that both pays at least part of training costs and does not pay market wages to skilled personnel. It has had, in consequence, relatively easy access to "students" and heavy losses of "graduates." Indeed, its graduates make up the predominant part of the supply in several civilian occupations. For example, well over 90 per cent of United States commercial airline pilots received much of their training in the armed forces. The military, of course, is not a commercial organization judged by profits and losses and has had no difficulty surviving and even thriving.

What about the old argument that firms in competitive labor markets have no incentive to provide on-the-job training because trained workers would be bid away by other firms? Firms that train workers are supposed to impart external economies to other firms because the latter can use these workers free of any training charge. An analogy with research and development is often drawn since a firm developing a process that cannot be patented or kept secret would impart ex-

[11] See *Manpower Management and Compensation,* report of the Cordiner Committee, Washington, 1957, Vol. I, Chart 3, and the accompanying discussion. The military not only wants to eliminate the inverse relation but apparently would like to create a positive relation because they have such a large investment in heavily trained personnel. For a recent and excellent study, see Gorman C. Smith, "Differential Pay for Military Technicians," unpublished Ph.D. dissertation, Columbia University, 1964.

ternal economies to competitors. This argument and analogy would apply if firms were to pay training costs, for they would suffer a "capital loss" whenever trained workers were bid away by other firms. Firms can, however, shift training costs to trainees and have an incentive to do so when faced with competition for their services.[12]

The difference between investment in training and in research and development can be put very simply. Without patents or secrecy, firms in competitive industries may have difficulty establishing property rights in innovations, and these innovations may become fair game for all comers. Patent systems try to establish these rights so that incentives can be provided to invest in research. Property rights in skills, on the other hand, are automatically vested, for a skill cannot be used without permission of the person possessing it. The property right of the worker in his skills is the source of his incentive to invest in training by accepting a reduced wage during the training period and explains why an analogy with unowned innovations is misleading.

SPECIFIC TRAINING

Completely general training increases the marginal productivity of trainees by exactly the same amount in the firms providing the training as in other firms. Clearly some kinds of training increase productivity by different amounts in the firms providing the training and in other firms. Training that increases productivity more in firms providing it will be called specific training. Completely specific training can be defined as training that has no effect on the productivity of trainees that would be useful in other firms. Much on-the-job training is neither completely specific nor completely general but increases productivity more in the firms providing it and falls within the definition of specific training. The rest increases productivity by at least as much in other firms and falls within a definition of general training. A few

---

[12] Sometimes the alleged external economies from on-the-job training have been considered part of the "infant industry" argument for protection (see J. Black "Arguments for Tariffs," *Oxford Economic Papers*, June 1959, pp. 205-206). Our analysis suggests, however, that the trouble tariffs are supposed to overcome must be traced back to difficulties that workers have in financing investment in themselves—in other words, to ignorance or capital market limitations that apply to expenditures on education, health, as well as on-the-job training. Protection would serve the same purpose as the creation of monopsonies domestically, namely, to convert general into specific capital so that firms can be given an incentive to pay for training (see the remarks on specific training below and in section 4 of this chapter). Presumably a much more efficient solution would be to improve the capital market directly through insurance of loans, subsidies, information, etc.

illustrations of the scope of specific training are presented before a formal analysis is developed.

The military offers some forms of training that are extremely useful in the civilian sector, as already noted, and others that are only of minor use to civilians, i.e., astronauts, fighter pilots, and missile men. Such training falls within the scope of specific training because productivity is raised in the military but not (much) elsewhere.

Resources are usually spent by firms in familiarizing new employees with their organization,[13] and the knowledge thus acquired is a form of specific training because productivity is raised more in the firms acquiring the knowledge than in other firms. Other kinds of hiring costs, such as employment agency fees, the expenses incurred by new employees in finding jobs, or the time employed in interviewing, testing, checking references, and in bookkeeping do not so obviously increase the knowledge of new employees, but they too are a form of specific investment in human capital, although not training. They are an investment because outlays over a short period create distributed effects on productivity; they are specific because productivity is raised primarily in the firms making the outlays; they are in human capital because they lose their value whenever employees leave. In the rest of this section reference is mostly to on-the-job specific training even though the analysis applies to all on-the-job specific investment.

Even after hiring costs are incurred, firms usually know only a limited amount about the ability and potential of new employees. They try to increase their knowledge in various ways—testing, rotation among departments, trial and error, etc.—for greater knowledge permits a more efficient utilization of manpower. Expenditures on acquiring knowledge of employee talents would be a specific investment if the knowledge could be kept from other firms, for then productivity would be raised more in the firms making the expenditures than elsewhere.

The effect of investment in employees on their productivity elsewhere depends on market conditions as well as on the nature of the investment. Very strong monopsonists might be completely insulated from competition by other firms, and practically all investments in their labor force would be specific. On the other hand, firms in ex-

---

[13] To judge from a sample of firms recently analyzed, formal orientation courses are quite common, at least in large firms (see H. F. Clark and H. S. Sloan, *Classrooms in the Factories,* New York, 1958, Chap. IV).

tremely competitive labor markets would face a constant threat of raiding and would have fewer specific investments available.

These examples convey some of the surprisingly large variety of situations that come under the rubric of specific investment. This set is now treated abstractly in order to develop a general formal analysis. Empirical situations are brought in again after several major implications of the formal analysis have been developed.

If all training were completely specific, the wage that an employee could get elsewhere would be independent of the amount of training he had received. One might plausibly argue, then, that the wage paid by firms would also be independent of training. If so, firms would have to pay training costs, for no rational employee would pay for training that did not benefit him. Firms would collect the return from such training in the form of larger profits resulting from higher productivity, and training would be provided whenever the return—discounted at an appropriate rate—was at least as large as the cost. Long-run competitive equilibrium requires that the present value of the return exactly equals costs.

These propositions can be stated more formally with the equations developed earlier. According to equations (5) and (7), the equilibrium of a firm providing training in competitive markets can be written as

$$MP_0' + G\left[= \sum_{t=1}^{n-1} \frac{MP_t - W_t}{(1+i)^t} \right] = W_0 + C, \qquad (11)$$

where C is the cost of training given only in the initial period, MP_0' is the opportunity marginal product of trainees, W_0 is the wage paid to trainees, and W_t and MP_t are the wage and marginal product in period t. If the analysis of completely specific training given in the preceding paragraph is correct, W would always equal the wage that could be received elsewhere, $MP_t - W_t$ would be the full return in t from training given in 0, and G would be the present value of these returns. Since MP_0' measures the marginal product elsewhere and W_0 measures the wage elsewhere of trainees, MP_0' equals W_0. As a consequence G equals C, or, in full equilibrium, the return from training equals costs.

Before claiming that the usual equality between marginal product and wages holds when completely specific training is considered, the reader should bear in mind two points. The first is that the equality between wages and marginal product in the initial period involves opportunity, not actual marginal product. Wages would be greater than actual marginal product if some productivity was foregone as part of the training program. The second is that, even if wages equaled marginal product initially, they would be less in the future because the differences between future marginal products and wages constitute the return to training and are collected by the firm.

All of this follows from the assumption that firms pay all costs and collect all returns. But could not one equally well argue that workers pay all specific training costs by receiving appropriately lower wages initially and collect all returns by receiving wages equal to marginal product later? In terms of equation (11), W_t would equal MP_t, G would equal zero, and W_0 would equal $MP_0' - C$, just as with general training. Is it more plausible that firms rather than workers pay for and collect and return from training?

An answer can be found by reasoning along the following lines. If a firm had paid for the specific training of a worker who quit to take another job, its capital expenditure would be partly wasted, for no further return could be collected. Likewise, a worker fired after he had paid for specific training would be unable to collect any further return and would also suffer a capital loss. The willingness of workers or firms to pay for specific training should, therefore, closely depend on the likelihood of labor turnover.

To bring in turnover at this point may seem like a *deus ex machina* since it is almost always ignored in traditional theory. In the usual analysis of competitive firms, wages equal marginal product, and since wages and marginal product are assumed to be the same in many firms, no one suffers from turnover. It would not matter whether a firm's labor force always contained the same persons or a rapidly changing group. Any person leaving one firm could do equally well in other firms, and his employer could replace him without any change in profits. In other words, turnover is ignored in traditional theory because it plays no important role within the framework of the theory.

Turnover becomes important when costs are imposed on workers or firms, which are precisely the effects of specific training. Suppose a firm paid all the specific training costs of a worker who quit after completing it. According to our earlier analysis, he would have been receiving the market wage and a new employee could be hired at the same wage. If the new employee were not given training, his marginal product would be less than that of the one who quit since presumably training raised the latter's productivity. Training could raise the new employee's productivity but would require additional expenditures by the firm. In other words, a firm is hurt by the departure of a trained employee because an equally profitable new employee could not be obtained. In the same way an employee who pays for specific training would suffer a loss from being laid off because he could not find an equally good job elsewhere. To bring turnover into the analysis of specific training is not, therefore, a *deus ex machina* but is made necessary by the important link between them.

Firms paying for specific training might take account of turnover merely by obtaining a sufficiently large return from those remaining to counterbalance the loss from those leaving. (The return on "successes"—those remaining—would, of course, overestimate the average return on all training expenditures.) Firms could do even better, however, by recognizing that the likelihood of a quit is not fixed but depends on wages. Instead of merely recouping on successes what is lost on failures, they might reduce the likelihood of failure itself by offering higher wages after training than could be received elsewhere. In effect, they would offer employees some of the return from training. Matters would be improved in some respects but worsened in others, for the higher wage would make the supply of trainees greater than the demand, and rationing would be required. The final step would be to shift some training costs as well as returns to employees, thereby bringing supply more in line with demand. When the final step is completed, firms no longer pay all training costs nor do they collect all the return but they share both with employees.[14] The shares of each depend on the relations between quit rates and wages, layoff rates and profits, and on other factors not discussed here, such as the cost of funds, attitudes toward risk, and desires for liquidity.[15]

[14] A. Marshall *(Principles of Economics,* 8th ed., New York, 1949, p. 626) was clearly aware of specific talents and their effect on wages and productivity: "Thus the head clerk in a business has an acquaintance with men and things, the use of which he could in some cases sell at a high price to rival firms. But in other cases it is of a kind to be of no value save to the business in which he already is; and *then his departure would perhaps injure it by several times the value of his salary,* while probably he could not get half that *salary elsewhere."* (My italics.) However, he overstressed the element of indeterminacy in these wages ("their earnings are determined . . . by a bargain between them and their employers, the terms of which are theoretically arbitrary") because he ignored the effect of wages on turnover *(ibid.,* fn. 2).

[15] The rate used to discount costs and returns is the sum of a (positive) rate measuring the cost of funds, a (positive or negative) risk premium, and a liquidity premium that is presumably positive since capital invested in specific training is very illiquid (see the discussion in section 2 of Chapter III).

If training were not completely specific, productivity would increase in other firms as well, and the wage that could be received elsewhere would also increase. Such training can be looked upon as the sum of two components, one completely general, the other completely specific; the former would be relatively larger, the greater the effect on wages in other firms relative to the firms providing the training. Since firms do not pay any of the completely general costs and only part of the completely specific costs, the fraction of costs paid by firms would be inversely related to the importance of the general component, or positively related to the specificity of the training.

Our conclusions can be stated formally in terms of the equations developed earlier. If G is the present value of the return from training collected by firms, the fundamental equation is

$$MP' + G = W + C. \tag{12}$$

If G' measures the return collected by employees, the total return, G'', would be the sum of G and G'. In full equilibrium the total return would equal total costs, or $G'' = C$. Let a represent the fraction of the total return collected by firms. Since $G = aG''$ and $G'' = C$, equation (12) can be written as

$$MP' + aC = W + C, \tag{13}$$

or

$$W = MP' - (1 - a)C.\text{[16]} \tag{14}$$

Employees pay the same fraction of costs, $1 - a$, as they collect in returns, which generalizes the results obtained earlier. For if training were completely general, $a = 0$, and equation (14) reduces to equation (10); if firms collected all the return from training, $a = 1$, and (14) reduces to $MP_0' = W_0$; and if $0 < a < 1$, none of the earlier equations is satisfactory.

A few major implications of this analysis of specific training are now developed.

---

[16] If G'' did not equal C, these equations would be slightly more complicated. Suppose, for example, $G'' = G + G' = C + n, n \geq 0$, so that the present value of the total return would be greater than total costs. Then $G = aG'' = aC + an$, and

$$MP' + aC + an = W + C,$$

or

$$W = MP' - [(1 - a)C - an].$$

Rational firms pay generally trained employees the same wage and specifically trained employees a higher wage than they could get elsewhere. A reader might easily believe the contrary—namely, that general training would command a higher wage relative to alternatives than specific training does, since, after all, competition for persons with the latter is apt to be weaker than for those with the former. This view, however, overlooks the fact that general training raises the wages that could be received elsewhere while (completely) specific training does not, so a comparison with alternative wages gives a misleading impression of the *absolute* effect on wages of different types of training. Moreover, firms are not too concerned about the turnover of employees with general training and have no incentive to offer them a premium above wages elsewhere because the cost of such training is borne entirely by employees. Firms are concerned about the turnover of employees with specific training, and a premium is offered to reduce their turnover because firms pay part of their training costs.

The part of specific training paid by employees has effects similar to those discussed earlier for general training: it is also paid by a reduction in wages during the training period, tends to make age-earnings profiles steeper and more concave, etc. The part paid by firms has none of these implications, since current or future wages would not be affected.

Specific, unlike general, training produces certain "external" effects, for quits prevent firms from capturing the full return on costs paid by them, and layoffs do the same to employees. These, however, are external *diseconomies* imposed on the employees or employers of firms providing the training, not external economies accruing to other firms.

Employees with specific training have less incentive to quit, and firms have less incentive to fire them, than employees with no training or general training, which implies that quit and layoff rates are inversely related to the amount of specific training. Turnover should be least for employees with extremely specific training and most for those receiving such general training that productivity is raised less in the firms providing the training than elsewhere (as, say, in schools). These propositions are as applicable to the large number of irregular quits and layoffs that continually occur as to the more regular cyclical and secular movements in turnover; in this section, however, only the more regular movements are discussed.

Consider a firm that experiences an unexpected decline in demand for its output, the rest of the economy being unaffected. The marginal product of employees without specific training—such as untrained or generally trained employees—presumably equaled wages initially, and their employment would now be reduced to prevent their marginal productivity from falling below wages. The marginal product of specifically trained employees initially would have been greater than wages. A decline in demand would reduce these marginal products too, but as long as they were reduced by less than the initial difference with wages, firms would have no incentive to lay off such employees. For sunk costs are sunk, and there is no incentive to lay off employees whose marginal product is greater than wages, no matter how unwise it was, in retrospect, to invest in their training. Thus workers with specific training seem less likely to be laid off as a consequence of a decline in demand than untrained or even generally trained workers.[17]

If the decline in demand were sufficiently great so that even the marginal product of specifically trained workers was pushed below wages, would the firm just proceed to lay them off until the marginal product was brought into equality with wages? To show the danger here, assume that all the cost of and return from specific training was paid and collected by the firm. Any worker laid off would try to find a new job, since nothing would bind him to the old one.[18] The firm might be hurt if he did find a new job, for the firm's investment in his training might be lost forever. If specifically trained workers were not laid off, the firm would lose now because marginal product would be less than wages but would gain in the future if the decline in demand proved temporary. There is an incentive, therefore, not to lay off workers with specific training when their marginal product is only temporarily below wages, and the larger a firm's investment the greater the incentive not to lay them off.

A worker collecting some of the return from specific training would have less incentive to find a new job when temporarily laid off than others would: he does not want to lose his investment. His behavior while laid off in turn affects his future chances of being laid off, for

---

[17] A very similar argument is developed by Walter Oi in "Labor as a Quasi-fixed Factor of Production," unpublished Ph.D. dissertation, University of Chicago, 1961. Also, see his article with almost the same title in *Journal of Political Economy*, December 1962.

[18] Actually one need only assume that the quit rate of laid-off workers tends to be significantly greater than that of employed workers, if only because the opportunity cost of searching for another job is less for laid-off workers.

if it were known that he would not readily take another job, the firm could lay him off without much fear of losing its investment.

These conclusions can be briefly summarized. If one firm alone experienced an unexpected decline in demand, relatively few workers with specific training would be laid off, if only because their marginal product was initially greater than their wage. If the decline were permanent, all workers would be laid off when their marginal product became less than their wage and all those laid off would have to find jobs elsewhere. If the decline were temporary, specifically trained workers might not be laid off even though their marginal product was less than their wage because the firm would suffer if they took other jobs. The likelihood of their taking other jobs would be inversely related, and therefore the likelihood of their being laid off would be positively related, to the extent of their own investment in training.

The analysis can easily be extended to cover general declines in demand; suppose, for example, a general cyclical decline occurred. Assume that wages were sticky and remained at the initial level. If the decline in business activity were not sufficient to reduce the marginal product below the wage, workers with specific training would not be laid off even though others would be, just as before. If the decline reduced marginal product below wages, only one modification in the previous analysis is required. A firm would have a greater incentive to lay off specifically trained workers than when it alone experienced a decline because laid-off workers would be less likely to find other jobs when unemployment was widespread. In other respects, the implications of a general decline with wage rigidity are the same as those of a decline in one firm alone.

The discussion has concentrated on layoff rates, but the same kind of reasoning shows that a rise in wages elsewhere would cause fewer quits among specifically trained workers than among others. For specifically trained workers initially receive higher wages than are available elsewhere and the wage rise elsewhere would have to be greater than the initial difference before they would consider quitting. Thus both the quit and layoff rate of specifically trained workers would be relatively low and fluctuate relatively less during business cycles. These are important implications that can be tested with the data available.

Although quits and layoffs are influenced by considerations other than investment costs, some of these, such as pension plans, are more strongly related to investments than may appear at first blush. A pension plan with incomplete vesting privileges[19] penalizes employees who quit before retirement and thus provides an incentive—often an extremely powerful one—not to quit. At the same time pension plans "insure" firms against quits for they are given a lump sum—the non-vested portion of payments—whenever a worker quits. Insurance is needed for specifically trained employees because their turnover would impose capital losses on firms. Firms can discourage such quits by sharing training costs and the return with employees, but they would have less need to discourage them and would be more willing to pay for training costs if insurance were provided. The effects on the incentive to invest in one's employees may have been a major stimulus to the development of pension plans with incomplete vesting.[20]

An effective long-term contract would insure firms against quits, just as pensions do and also insure employees against layoffs. Firms would be more willing to pay for all kinds of training—assuming future wages were set at an appropriate level—since a contract, in effect, converts all training into completely specific training. A casual reading of history suggests that long-term contracts have, indeed, been primarily a means of inducing firms to undertake large investments in employees. These contracts are seldom used today in the United States,[21] and while they have declined in importance over time, they were probably always the exception here largely because courts have considered them a form of involuntary servitude. Moreover, any enforcible contract could at best specify the hours required on a job, not the quality of performance. Since performance can vary widely, unhappy workers could usually "sabotage" operations to induce employers to release them from contracts.

Some training may be useful not in most firms nor in a single firm, but in a set of firms defined by product, type of work, or geographical location. For example, carpentry training would raise productivity primarily in the construction industry, and French legal training would not be very useful in the United States. Such training would tend to be paid by trainees, since a single firm could not readily col-

19 According to the as yet unpublished National Bureau study of pensions, most plans have incomplete vesting.

20 This economic function of incomplete vesting should caution one against conceding to the agitation for more liberal vesting privileges. Of course, in recent years pensions have also been an important tax-saving device, which certainly has been a crucial factor in their mushrooming growth.

21 The military and the entertainment industry are the major exceptions.

lect the return,[22] and in this respect would be the same as general training. In one respect, however, it is similar to specific training. Workers with training "specific" to an industry, occupation, or country are less likely to leave that industry, occupation, or country than other workers, so their industrial, occupational, or country "turnover" would be less than average. The same result is obtained for specific training, except that a firm rather than an industry, occupation, or country is used as the unit of observation in measuring turnover. An analysis of specific training, therefore, is helpful also in understanding the effects of certain types of "general" training.

Although a discrepancy between marginal product and wages is frequently taken as evidence of imperfections in the competitive system, it would occur even in a perfectly competitive system where there is investment in specific training. The investment approach provides a very different interpretation of some common phenomena, as can be seen from the following examples.

A positive difference between marginal product and wages is usually said to be evidence of monopsony power; just as the ratio of product price to marginal cost has been suggested as a measure of monopoly power, so has the ratio of marginal product to wages been suggested as a measure of monopsony power. But specific training would also make this ratio greater than one. Does the difference between the marginal product and the earnings of major-league baseball players, for example, measure monopsony power or the return on a team's investment? Since teams do spend a great deal on developing players, some and perhaps most of the difference must be considered a return on investment (even if there were no uncertainty about the abilities of different players).[23]

Earnings might differ greatly among firms, industries, and countries and yet there might be relatively little worker mobility. The usual explanation would be that workers were either irrational or faced with formidable obstacles in moving. However, if specific[24] training

22 Sometimes firms cooperate in paying training costs, especially when training apprentices (see *A Look at Industrial Training in Mercer County, N. J.*, Washington, 1959, p. 3).

23 S. Rottenberg ("The Baseball Players' Labor Market," *Journal of Political Economy*, June 1956, p. 254) argues that the strong restrictions on entry of teams into the major leagues is prima-facie evidence that monopsony power is important, but the entry or threat of new *leagues*, such as have occurred in professional basketball and football, is a real possibility. And, of course, new teams have entered in recent years.

24 Specific, that is, to the firms, industries, or countries in question.

were important, differences in earnings would be a misleading estimate of what "migrants" could receive, and it might be perfectly
rational not to move. For example, although French lawyers earn less
than American lawyers, the average French lawyer could not earn the
average American legal income simply by migrating to the United
States, for he would have to invest in learning English and American
law and procedures.[25]

In extreme types of monopsony, exemplified by an isolated company town, job alternatives for both trained and untrained workers
are nil, and all training, no matter what its nature, would be specific
to the firm. Monopsony combined with control of a product or an
occupation (due, say, to antipirating agreements) converts training
specific to that product or occupation into firm-specific training.
These kinds of monopsony increase the importance of specific training and thus the incentive to invest in employees.[26] The effect on
training of less extreme monopsony positions is more difficult assess.
Consider the monopsonist who pays his workers the best wage available elsewhere. I see no reason why training should have a systematically different effect on the foregone earnings of his employees than
of those in competitive firms and, therefore, no reason why specific
training should be more (or less) important to him. But monopsony
power as a whole, including the more extreme manifestations, would
appear to increase the importance of specific training and the incentive for firms to invest in human capital.

2. Schooling

A school can be defined as an institution specializing in the production of training, as distinct from a firm that offers training in conjunction with the production of goods. Some schools, like those for
barbers, specialize in one skill, while others, like universities, offer a
large and diverse set. Schools and firms are often substitute sources of
particular skills. This substitution is evidenced by the shift over time,

25 Of course, persons who have not yet invested in themselves would have an incentive to migrate, and this partly explains why young persons migrate more than older
ones. For a further explanation, see the discussion in Chapter III; also see the paper
by L. Sjaastad, "The Costs and Returns of Human Migration," *Investment in Human
Beings*, pp. 80-93.
26 A relatively large difference between marginal product and wages in monopsonies
might measure, therefore, the combined effect of economic power and a relatively large
investment in employees.

for instance, in law from apprenticeships in law firms to law schools and in engineering from on-the-job experience to engineering schools.[27]

Some types of knowledge can be mastered better if simultaneously related to a practical problem; others require prolonged specialization. That is, there are complementary elements between learning and work and between learning and time. Most training in the construction industry is apparently still best given on the job, while the training of physicists requires a long period of specialized effort. The development of certain skills requires both specialization and experience and can be had partly from firms and partly from schools. Physicians receive apprenticeship training as interns and residents after several years of concentrated instruction in medical schools. Or, to take an example closer to home, a research economist spends not only many years in school but also a rather extensive apprenticeship in mastering the "art" of empirical and theoretical research. The complementary elements between firms and schools depend in part on the amount of formalized knowledge available: price theory can be formally presented in a course, while a formal statement of the principles used in gathering and handling empirical materials is lacking. Training in a new industrial skill is usually first given on the job, since firms tend to be the first to be aware of its value, but as demand develops, some of the training shifts to schools.

A student does not work for pay while in school but may do so after or before school, or during vacations. His earnings are usually less than if he were not in school since he cannot work as much or as regularly. The difference between what could have been and what is earned (including any value placed on foregone leisure) is an important indirect cost of schooling. Tuition, fees, books, supplies, and unusual transportation and lodging expenses are other, more direct, costs. *Net* earnings can be defined as the difference between actual earnings and direct school costs. In symbols,

$$W = MP - k, \qquad (15)$$

where MP is actual marginal product (assumed equal to earnings) and k is direct costs. If MP_0 is the marginal product that could have been received, equation (15) can be written as

$$W = MP_0 - (MP_0 - MP + k) = MP_0 - C, \qquad (16)$$

[27] State occupational licensing requirements often permit on-the-job training to be substituted for school training (see S. Rottenberg, "The Economics of Occupational Licensing," *Aspects of Labor Economics,* pp. 3-20).

where C is the sum of direct and indirect costs and where net earnings are the difference between potential earnings and total costs. These relations should be familiar since they are the same as those derived for general on-the-job training, which suggests that a sharp distinction between schools and firms is not always necessary: for some purposes schools can be treated as a special kind of firm and students as a special kind of trainee. Perhaps this is most apparent when a student works in an enterprise controlled by his school, which frequently occurs at many colleges.

Our definition of student net earnings may seem strange since tuition and other direct costs are not usually subtracted from "gross" earnings. Note, however, that indirect school costs are implicitly subtracted, for otherwise earnings would have to be defined as the sum of observed and foregone earnings, and foregone earnings are a major cost of high-school, college, and adult schooling. Moreover, earnings of on-the-job trainees would be net of *all* their costs, including direct "tuition" costs. Consistent accounting, which is particularly important when comparing earnings of persons trained in school and on the job, would require that earnings of students be defined in the same way.[28]

Regardless of whether all costs or merely indirect costs are subtracted from potential earnings, schooling would have the same kind of implications as general on-the-job training. Thus schooling would steepen the age-earnings profile, mix together the income and capital accounts, introduce a negative relation between the permanent and current earnings of young persons, and (implicitly) provide for depreciation on its capital. This supports my earlier assertion that an analysis of on-the-job training leads to general results that apply to other kinds of investment in human capital as well.

3. *Other Knowledge*

On-the-job and school training are not the only activities that raise real income primarily by increasing the knowledge at a person's command. Information about the prices charged by different sellers would enable a person to buy from the cheapest, thereby raising his command over resources; information about the wages offered by different firms would enable him to work for the firm paying the highest. In both examples, information about the economic system and about

[28] Students often have negative net earnings and in this respect differ from most on-the-job trainees, although at one time many apprentices also had negative earnings.

consumption and production possibilities is increased, as distinct from knowledge of a particular skill. Information about the political or social system—the effect of different parties or social arrangements— could also significantly raise real incomes.[29]

Let us consider in more detail investment in information about employment opportunities. A better job might be found by spending money on employment agencies and situation-wanted ads, by using one's time to examine want ads, by talking to friends and visiting firms, or in Stigler's language by "search."[30] When the new job re- quires geographical movement, additional time and resources would be spent in moving.[31] These expenditures constitute an investment in information about job opportunities that would yield a return in the form of higher earnings than would otherwise have been received. If workers paid the costs and collected the return, an investment in search would have the same implications about age-earnings profiles, depreciation, etc., as general on-the-job training and schooling, al- though it must be noted that the direct costs of search, like the direct costs of schooling, are usually added to consumption rather than deducted from earnings. If firms paid the costs and collected the return, search would have the same implications as on-the-job specific training.

Whether workers or firms pay for search depends on the effect of a job change on alternatives: the larger the number of alternatives made available by a change, the large (not the smaller) is the fraction of costs that have to be paid by workers. Consider a few examples. Immigrants to the United States have usually found many firms that could use their talents, and these firms would have been reluctant to pay the high cost of transporting workers to the United States. In fact immigrants have almost always had to pay their own way. Even a system of contract labor, which was seen to be a means of protecting firms against turnover, was singularly unsuccessful in the United

[29] The role of political knowledge is systematically discussed in A. Downs, *An Economic Theory of Democracy,* New York, 1957, and more briefly in my "Competition and Democracy," *Journal of Law and Economics,* October 1958.

[30] See G. J. Stigler, "Information in the Labor Market," *Investment in Human Beings,* pp. 94-105.

[31] Studies of large geographical moves—those requiring both a change in employ- ment and consumption—have tended to emphasize the job change more than the consumption change. Presumably money wages are considered to be more dispersed geographically than prices.

States and has been infrequently used.[32] Firms that are relatively insulated from competition in the labor market have an incentive to pay the costs of workers coming from elsewhere since they have little to worry about in the way of competing neighboring firms. In addition, firms would be willing partly to pay for search within a geographical area because some costs—such as an employment agency's fee—would be specific to the firm doing the hiring since they must be repeated at each job change.

4. Productive Wage Increases

One way to invest in human capital is to improve emotional and physical health. In Western countries today earnings are much more closely geared to knowledge than to strength, but in an earlier day, and elsewhere still today, strength had a significant influence on earnings. Moreover, emotional health increasingly is considered an important determinant of earnings in all parts of the world. Health, like knowledge, can be improved in many ways. A decline in the death rate at working ages may improve earning prospects by extending the period during which earnings are received; a better diet adds strength and stamina, and thus earning capacity; or an improvement in working conditions—higher wages, coffee breaks, and so on—may affect morale and productivity.

Firms can invest in the health of employees through medical examinations, lunches, or avoidance of activities with high accident and death rates. An investment in health that increased productivity to the same extent in many firms would be a general investment and would have the same effect as general training, while an investment in health that increased productivity more in the firms making it would be a specific investment and would have the same effect as specific training. Of course, most investments in health in the United States are made outside firms, in households, hospitals, and medical offices. A full analysis of the effect on earnings of such "outside" investment in health is beyond the scope of this study, but I would like to discuss a relation between on-the-job and "outside" human investments that has received much attention in recent years.

When on-the-job investments are paid by reducing earnings during

[32] For a careful discussion of the contract-labor system in the United States, see C. Erickson, *American Industry and the European Immigrant, 1860-1885,* Cambridge, Mass., 1957.

the investment period, less is available for investments outside the job in health, better diet, schooling, and other factors. If these "outside" investments were more productive, some on-the-job investments would not be undertaken even though they were very productive by "absolute" standards.

Before proceeding further, one point needs to be made. The amount invested outside the job would be related to current earnings only if the capital market was very imperfect, for otherwise any amount of 'outside" investment could be financed with borrowed funds. The analysis assumes, therefore, that the capital market is extremely imperfect, earnings and other income being a major source of funds.[33]

A firm would be willing to pay for investment in human capital made by employees outside the firm if it could benefit from the resulting increase in productivity. The only way to pay, however, would be to offer higher wages during the investment period than would have been offered since direct loans to employees are prohibited by assumption. When a firm gives a productive wage increase—that is, an increase that raises productivity—"outside" investments are, as it were, converted into on-the-job investments. Indeed, such a conversion is a natural way to circumvent imperfections in the capital market and the resultant dependence of the amount invested in human capital on the level of wages.

The discussion can be stated more formally. Let W represent wages in the absence of any investment, and let a productive wage increase costing an amount C be the only on-the-job investment. Total costs to the firm would be $\pi = W + C$, and since the investment cost is received by employees as higher wages, π would also measure total wages. The cost of on-the-job training is not received as higher wages, so this formally distinguishes a productive wage increase from other on-the-job investments. The term MP can represent the marginal product of employees when wages equal W, and G the gain to firms from the investment in higher wages. In full equilibrium,

$$MP + G = W + C = \pi. \tag{17}$$

Investment would not occur if the firm's gain was nil $(G = 0)$, for then total wages (π) would equal the marginal product (MP) when there is no investment.

[33] Imperfections in the capital market with respect to investment in human capital are discussed in section 2 of Chapter III.

Effects on Earnings

It has been shown that firms would benefit more from on-the-job investment the more specific the productivity effect, the greater their monopsony power, and the longer the labor contract; conversely, the benefit would be less the more general the productivity effect, the less their monopsony power, and the shorter the labor contract. For example, a wage increase spent on a better diet with an immediate impact on productivity might well be granted,[34] but not one spent on general education with a very delayed impact.[35]

The effect of a wage increase on productivity depends on the way it is spent, which in turn depends on tastes, knowledge, and opportunities. Firms might exert an influence on spending by exhorting employees to obtain good food, housing, and medical care, or even by requiring purchases of specified items in company stores. Indeed, the company store or truck system in nineteenth century Great Britain has been interpreted as partly designed to prevent an excessive consumption of liquor and other debilitating commodities.[36] The prevalance of employer paternalism in underdeveloped countries has frequently been accepted as evidence of a difference in temperament between East and West. An alternative interpretation suggested by our study is that an increase in consumption has a greater effect on productivity in underdeveloped countries, and that a productivity advance raises profits more there either because firms have more monopsony power or because the advance is less delayed. In other

[34] The more rapid the impact, the more likely it is that it comes within the (formal or de facto) contract period. Leibenstein apparently initially assumed a rapid impact when discussing wage increases in underdeveloped countries (see his "The Theory of Underemployment in Backward Economies," *Journal of Political Economy*, April 1957). In a later comment he argued that the impact might be delayed ("Underemployment in Backward Economies: Some Additional Notes," *Journal of Political Economy*, June 1958).

[35] Marshall *(Principles of Economics,* p. 566) discusses delays of a generation or more and notes that profit-maximizing firms in competitive industries have no incentive to grant such wage increases.

"Again, in paying his workpeople high wages and in caring for their happiness and culture, the liberal employer confers benefits which do not end with his own generation. For the children of his workpeople share in them, and grow up stronger in body and in character than otherwise they would have done. The price which he has paid for labour will have borne the expenses of production of an increased supply of high industrial faculties in the next generation: but these faculties will be the property of others, who will have the right to hire them out for the best price they will fetch: neither he nor even his heirs can reckon on reaping much material reward for this part of the good that he has done."

[36] See G. W. Hilton, "The British Truck System in the Nineteenth Century," *Journal of Political Economy*, April 1957, pp. 246-247.

words "paternalism" may simply be a way of investing in the health and welfare of employees in underdeveloped countries.

An investment in human capital would usually steepen age-earnings profiles, lowering reported earnings during the investment period and raising them later on. But an investment in an increase in earnings may have precisely the opposite effect, raising reported earnings more during the investment period than later and thus flattening age-earning profiles. The cause of this difference is simply that reported earnings during the investment period tend to be net of the cost of general investments and gross of the cost of an increase in productive earnings.[37]

The productivity of employees depends not only on their ability and the amount invested in them both on and off the job but also on their motivation, or the intensity of their work. Economists have long recognized that motivation in turn partly depends on earnings because of the effect of an increase in earnings on morale and aspirations. Equation (17), which was developed to show the effect of investments outside the firm financed by an increase in earnings, can also show the effect of an increase in the intensity of work "financed" by an increase in earnings. Thus W and MP would show initial earnings and productivity, C the increase in earnings, and G the gain to firms from the increase in productivity caused by the "morale" effect of the increase in earnings. The incentive to grant a morale-boosting increase in earnings, therefore, would depend on the same factors as does the incentive to grant an increase used for outside investments. Many recent discussions of wages in underdeveloped countries have stressed the latter,[38] while earlier discussions often stressed the former.[39]

[37] If E represents reported earnings during the investment period and MP the marginal product when there is no investment, $E = MP - C$ with a general investment, $E = MP$ with a specific investment paid by the firm, and $E = MP + C$ with an increase in productive earnings.

[38] See Leibenstein, *Journal of Political Economy*, April 1957, and H. Oshima, "Underdevelopment in Backward Economies: An Empirical Comment," *Journal of Political Economy*, June 1958.

[39] For example, Marshall stressed the effect of an increase in earnings on the character and habits of working people (*Principles of Economics*, pp. 529-532, 566-569).

CHAPTER III

Investment in Human Capital: Rates of Return

THE most important single determinant of the amount invested in human capital may well be its profitability or rate of return, but the effect on earnings of a change in the rate of return has been difficult to distinguish empirically from a change in the amount invested. For since investment in human capital usually extends over a long and variable period, the amount invested cannot be determined from a known "investment period." Moreover, the discussion of on-the-job training clearly indicated that the amount invested is often merged with gross earnings into a single net earnings concept (which is gross earnings minus the cost of or plus the return on investment).

1. Relation Between Earnings, Costs, and Rates of Return

In this section, some important relations between earnings, investment costs, and rates of return are derived. They permit one to distinguish, among other things, a change in the return from a change in the amount invested. The discussion proceeds in stages from simple to complicated situations. First, investment is restricted to a single period and returns to all remaining periods; then investment is distributed over a known group of periods called the investment period. Finally, it is shown how the rate of return, the amount invested, and the investment period can all be derived from information on net earnings alone.

The discussion is from the viewpoint of workers and is, therefore, restricted to general investments; since the analysis of specific investments and firms is very similar, its discussion is omitted.

Let Y be an activity providing a person entering at a particular age, called age zero, with a real net earnings stream of Y_0 during the first period, Y_1 during the next period, and so on until Y_n during the last period. The general term "activity" rather than occupation or another more concrete term is used in order to indicate that any kind of investment in human capital is permitted, not just on-the-job training but also schooling, information, health, and morale. As in the previous chapter, "net" earnings mean "gross" earnings during any period minus tuition costs during the same period. "Real" earnings are the sum of monetary earnings and the monetary equivalent of psychic earnings. Since many persons appear to believe that the term "investment in human capital" must be restricted to monetary costs and returns, let me emphasize that essentially the whole analysis applies independently of the division of real earnings into monetary and psychic components. Thus the analysis applies to health, which has a large psychic component, as well as to on-the-job training, which has a large monetary component. When psychic components dominate, the language associated with consumer durable goods might be considered more appropriate than that associated with investment goods; to simplify the presentation, investment language is used throughout.

The present value of the net earnings stream in Y would be

$$V(Y) = \sum_{j=0}^{n} \frac{Y_j}{(1+i)^{j+1}},^{1} \tag{18}$$

where i is the market discount rate, assumed for simplicity to be the same in each period. If X were another activity providing a net earning stream of X_0, X_1, . . . X_n, with a present value of $V(X)$, the present value of the gain from choosing Y would be given by

$$d = V(Y) - V(X) = \sum_{j=0}^{n} \frac{Y_j - X_j}{(1+i)^{j+1}}. \tag{19}$$

Equation (19) can be reformulated to bring out explicitly the relation between costs and returns. The cost of investing in human

[1] The discussion assumes discrete income flows and compounding, even though a mathematically more elegant formulation would have continuous variables, with sums replaced by integrals and discount rates by continuous compounding. The discrete approach is, however, easier to follow and yields the same kind of results. Extensions to the continuous case are straightforward.

capital equals the net earnings foregone by choosing to invest rather than choosing an activity requiring no investment. If activity Y requires an investment only in the initial period and if X does not require any, the cost of choosing Y rather than X is simply the difference between their net earnings in the initial period, and the total return would be the present value of the differences between net earnings in later periods. If $C = X_0 - Y_0$, $k_j = Y_j - X_j$, $j = 1, \ldots n$, and if R measures the total return, the gain from Y could be written as

$$d(1 + i) = \sum_{j=1}^{n} \frac{k_j}{(1 + i)^j} - C = R - C. \tag{20}$$

The relation between costs and returns can be derived in a different and, for our purposes, preferable way by defining the internal rate of return,[2] which is simply a rate of discount equating the present value of returns to the present value of costs. In other words, the internal rate, r, is defined implicitly by the equation

$$C = \sum_{1}^{n} \frac{k_j}{(1 + r)^j}, \tag{21}$$

which clearly implies

$$\sum_{j=0}^{n} \frac{Y_j}{(1 + r)^{j+1}} - \sum_{0}^{n} \frac{X_j}{(1 + r)^{j+1}} = d = 0, \tag{22}$$

since $C = X_0 - Y_0$ and $k_j = Y_j - X_j$. So the internal rate is also a rate of discount equating the present values of net earnings. These equations would be considerably simplified if the return were the same in each period, or $Y_j = X_j + k$, $j = 1, \ldots n$. Thus equation (21) would become

$$C = \frac{k}{r} [1 - (1 + r)^{-n}], \tag{23}$$

where $(1 + r)^{-n}$ is a correction for the finiteness of life that tends toward zero as people live longer.

[2] A substantial literature has developed on the difference between the income gain and internal return approaches. See, for example, Friedrich and Vera Lutz, *The Theory of Investment of the Firm,* Princeton, 1951, Chap. ii, and the articles in *The Management of Corporate Capital,* Ezra Solomon, ed., Glencoe, 1959.

If investment is restricted to a single known period, cost and rate of return are easily determined from information on net earnings alone. Since investment in human capital is distributed over many periods—formal schooling is usually more than ten years in the United States, and long periods of on-the-job training are also common—the analysis must, however, be generalized to cover distributed investment. The definition of an internal rate in terms of the present value of net earnings in different activities obviously applies regardless of the amount and duration of investment, but the definition in terms of costs and returns is not generalized so readily. If investment were known to occur in Y during each of the first m periods, a simple and superficially appealing approach would be to define the investment cost in each of these periods as the difference between net earnings in X and Y, total investment costs as the present value of these differences, and the internal rate would equate total costs and returns. In symbols,

$$C_j^1 = X_j - Y_j, j = 0, \ldots m - 1,$$

$$C^1 = \sum_0^{m-1} C_j^1 (1 + r)^{-j},$$

and

$$C^1 = \frac{k}{r} \frac{(1 - (1 + r)^{m-1-n})}{(1 + r)^{m-1}}. \tag{24}$$

If $m = 1$, this reduces to equation (23).

Two serious drawbacks mar this appealing straightforward approach. The estimate of total costs requires a priori knowledge and specification of the investment period. While the period covered by formal schooling is easily determined, the period covered by much on-the-job training and other investment is not, and a serious error might result from an incorrect specification: to take an extreme example, total costs would approach zero as the investment period is assumed to be longer and longer.[3]

[3] Since

$$C^1 = \sum_0^{m-1} (X_j - Y_j) (1 + r)^{-j}, \lim_{m \to n} C^1 = \sum_0^{n-1} (X_j - Y_j) (1 + r)^{-j} = 0,$$

by definition of the internal rate.

A second difficulty is that the differences between net earnings in X and Y do not correctly measure the cost of investing in Y since they do not correctly measure earnings foregone. A person who invested in the initial period could receive more than X_1 in period 1 as long as the initial investment yielded a positive return.[4] The true cost of an investment in period 1 would be the total earnings foregone, or the difference between what could have been received and what is received. The difference between X_1 and Y_1 could greatly underestimate true costs; indeed, Y_1 might be greater than X_1 even though a large investment was made in period 1.[5] In general, therefore, the amount invested in any period would be determined not only from net earnings in the same period but also from net earnings in earlier periods.

If the cost of an investment is consistently defined as the earnings foregone, quite different estimates of total costs emerge. Although superficially a less natural and straightforward approach, the generalization from a single period to distributed investment is actually greatly simplified. Therefore, let C_j be the foregone earnings in the jth period, r_j the rate of return on C_j, and let the return per period on C_j be a constant k_j, with $k = \Sigma k_j$ being the total return on the whole investment. If the number of periods were indefinitely large, and if investment occured only in the first m periods, the equation relating costs, returns, and internal rates would have the strikingly simple form of[6]

[4] If C_0 was the initial investment, r_0 its internal rate, and if the return were the same in all years, the amount

$$X_1^1 = X_1 + \frac{r_0 C_0}{1 - (1 + r_0)^{-n}}$$

could be received in period 1.

[5] Y_1 is greater than X_1 if

$$X_1 + \frac{r_0 C_0}{1 - (1 + r_0)^{-n}} - C_1 > X_1, \text{ or if } \frac{r_0 C_0}{1 - (1 + r_0)^{-n}} > C_1,$$

where C_1 is the investment in period 1.

[6] A proof is straightforward. An investment in period j would yield a return of the amount $k_j = r_j C_j$ in each succeeding period if the number of periods were infinite and the return were the same in each. Since the total return is the sum of individual returns,

$$k = \sum_0^{m-1} k_j = \sum_0^{m-1} r_j C_j = C \sum_0^{m-1} \frac{r_j C_j}{C} = \bar{r} C.$$

I am indebted to Helen Raffel for important suggestions which led to this simple proof.

$$C = \sum_{0}^{m-1} C_j = \frac{k}{\bar{r}}, \qquad (25)$$

where

$$\bar{r} = \sum_{0}^{m-1} w_j r_j, \quad w_j = \frac{C_j}{C},$$

and

$$\sum_{0}^{m-1} w_j = 1. \qquad (26)$$

Total cost, defined simply as the sum of costs during each period, would equal the capitalized value of returns, the rate of capitalization being a weighted average of the rates of return on the individual investments. Any sequence of internal rates or investment costs is permitted, no matter what the pattern of rises and declines, or the form of investments, be they a college education, an apprenticeship, ballet lessons, or a medical examination. Different investment programs would have the same ultimate effect on earnings whenever the average rate of return and the sum of investment costs were the same.[7]

Equation (25) could be given an interesting interpretation if all rates of return were the same. The term k/r would then be the value at the beginning of the mth period of all succeeding net earning differentials between Y and X discounted at the internal rate, r.[8] Total costs would equal the value also at the beginning of the mth period—which is the end of the investment period—of the first m differentials between X and Y.[9] The value of the first m differentials between X

[7] Note that the rate of return equating the present values of net earnings in X and Y is not necessarily equal to $\bar{r}$, for it would weight the rates of return on earlier investments more heavily than $\bar{r}$ does. For example, if rates were higher on investments in earlier than in later periods, the over-all rate would be greater than $\bar{r}$, and vice versa if rates were higher in later periods. Sample calculations indicate, however, that the difference between the over-all rate and $\bar{r}$ tends to be small as long as the investment period was not very long and the systematic difference between internal rates not very great.

[8] That is,

$$\sum_{j=m}^{\infty} (Y_j - X_j)(1+r)^{m-1-i} = k \sum_{m}^{\infty} (1+r)^{m-1-i} = \frac{k}{r}.$$

[9] Since, by definition,

$$X_0 - Y_0 = C_0, \quad X_1 - Y_1 = C_1 - rC_0,$$

and Y must equal the value of all succeeding differentials between Y and X, since r would be the rate of return equating the present values in X and Y.

The internal rate of return and the amount invested in each of the first m periods could be estimated from the net earnings streams in X and Y alone if the rate of return were the same on all investments. For the internal rate r could be determined from the condition that the present value of net earnings must be the same in X and Y, and the amount invested in each period seriatim from the relations[10]

$$C_0 = X_0 - Y_0, \quad C_1 = X_1 - Y_1 + rC_0$$

$$\tag{27}$$

$$C_j = X_j - Y_j + r \sum_{k=0}^{j-1} C_k, \ 0 \le j \le m - 1.^{[11]}$$

and more generally

then
$$X_j - Y_j = C_j - r \sum_{k=0}^{j-1} C_k, \quad 0 \le j < m,$$

$$\sum_{j=0}^{m-1} (X_j - Y_j)(1+r)^{m-1-j} = \sum_{j=0}^{m-1} \left(C_j - r \sum_{0}^{j-1} C_k \right)(1+r)^{m-1-j}$$

$$= \sum_{0}^{m-1} C_j \left\{ (1+r)^{m-1-j} - r[1 + (1+r) + \cdots + (1+r)^{m-2-j}] \right\}$$

$$= \sum_{0}^{m-1} C_j = C.$$

The analytical difference between the naive definition of costs advanced earlier and one in terms of foregone earnings is that the former measures total costs by the value of earning differentials at the beginning of the investment period and the latter by the value at the end of the period. Therefore, $C^1 = C(1 + r)^{1-m}$, which follows from eq. (24) when $n = \infty$.

[10] If the rate of return were not the same on all investments there would be $2m$ unknowns—$C_0, \ldots C_{m-1}$, and $r_0, \ldots r_{m-1}$—and only $m + 1$ equations—the m cost definitions and the equation

$$Y_p - X_p = k = \sum_{0}^{m+1} r_i C_i, p \ge m.$$

An additional $m - 1$ relation would be required to determine the $2m$ unknowns. The condition $r_0 = r_1 = \ldots = r_{m-1}$ is only one form these $m - 1$ relations can take; another is that costs decrease at certain known rates. If the latter were assumed, all the r_i could be determined from the earnings data.

[11] In econometric terminology this set of equations forms a "causal chain" because of the natural time ordering provided by the aging process. Consequently, there is no identification or "simultaneity" problem.

Thus costs and the rate of return can be estimated from information on net earnings. This is fortunate since the return on human capital is never empirically separated from other earnings and the cost of such capital is only sometimes and incompletely separated.

The investment period of education can be measured by years of schooling, but the periods of on-the-job training, of the search for information, and of other investments are not readily available. Happily, one need not know the investment period to estimate costs and returns, since all three can be simultaneously estimated from information on net earnings. If activity X were known to have no investment (a zero investment period), the amount invested in Y during any period would be defined by

$$C_j = X_j - Y_j + r \sum_0^{j-1} C_k, \text{ all } j, \tag{28}$$

and total costs by

$$C = \sum_0^{\infty} C_j. \tag{29}$$

The internal rate could be determined in the usual way from the equality between present values in X and Y, costs in each period from equation (28), and total costs from equation (29).

The definition of costs presented here simply extends to all periods the definition advanced earlier for the investment period.[12] The

[12] Therefore, since the value of the first m earning differentials has been shown to equal

$$\sum_0^{m-1} C_j$$

at period m (see footnote 9), total costs could be estimated from the value of all differentials at the end of the earning period. That is,

$$C = \sum_0^{\infty} C_j = \sum_0^{\infty} (X_j - Y_j)^{\infty-1-j}.$$

Thus the value of all differentials would equal zero at the beginning of the earning period—by definition of the internal rate—and C at the end. The apparent paradox results from the infinite horizon, as can be seen from the following equation relating the value of the first f differentials at the beginning of the gth period to costs:

44

rationale for the general definition is the same: investment occurs in Y whenever earnings there are below the sum of those in X and the income accruing on prior investments. If costs were found to be greater than zero before some period m and equal to zero thereafter, the first m periods would be the empirically derived investment period. But costs and returns can be estimated from equation (28) even when there is no simple investment period.

A common objection to an earlier draft of this paper was that the general and rather formal definition of costs advanced here is all right when applied to on-the-job training, schooling, and other recognized investments, but goes too far by also including as investment costs many effects that should be treated otherwise.

Thus, so the protest might run, learning would automatically lead to a convex and relatively steep earnings profile not because of any associated investment in education or training, but because the well-known "learning curve" is usually convex and rather steep. Since the method presented here, however, depends only on the shape of age-earnings profiles, the effect of learning would be considered an effect of investment in human capital. I accept the argument fully; indeed, I believe that it points up the power rather than the weakness of my analysis and the implied concept of human capital.

To see this requires a fuller analysis of the effect of learning. Assume that Z permits learning and that another activity X does not and has a flat earnings profile: Z might have the profile labeled TT in Chart 1 (in Chapter II) and X that labeled UU. If TT were everywhere above UU—i.e., earnings in Z were greater than those in X at each age—there would be a clear incentive for some persons to leave X and enter Z. The result would be a lowering of TT and raising of UU; generally the process would continue until TT was no longer everywhere above UU, as in Chart 1. Earnings would now be lower in Z than in X at younger ages and higher only later on, and workers

---

$$V\,(f, g) = \sum_{j=0}^{f-1} (X_j - Y_j)\,(1 + r)^{g-1-j} = \sum_{j=0}^{f-1} C_j(1 + r)^{g-f}.$$

When $f = \infty$ and $g = 0$, $V = 0$, but whenever $f = g$,

$$V = \sum_{0}^{f-1} C_j.$$

In particular, if $f = g = \infty$, $V = C$.

would have to decide whether the later higher earnings compensated for the lower initial earnings.

They presumably would decide by comparing the present value of earnings in Z and X, or, what is equivalent, by comparing the rate of return that equates these present values with rates that could be obtained elsewhere. They would choose Z if the present value were greater there, or if the equalizing rate were greater than those elsewhere. Therefore, they would choose Z only if the rate of return on their learning were sufficiently great, i.e., only if the returns from learning—the higher earnings later on—offset the costs of learning—the lower earnings initially. Thus choosing between activities "with a future" and "dead-end" activities involves exactly the same considerations as choosing between continuing one's education and entering the labor force—whether returns in the form of higher subsequent earnings sufficiently offset costs in the form of lower initial ones. Although learning cannot be avoided once in activities like Z, it can be avoided beforehand because workers can enter activities like X that provide little or no learning. They or society would choose learning only if it were a sufficiently good investment in the same way that they or society would choose on-the-job training if it were sufficiently profitable.

Consequently, the conclusion must be that learning is a way to invest in human capital that is formally no different from education, on-the-job training, or other recognized investments. So it is a virtue rather than a defect of our formulation of costs and returns that learning is treated symmetrically with other investments. And there is no conflict between interpretations of the shape of earning profiles based on learning theory[13] and those based on investment in human capital because the former is a special case of the latter. Of course, the fact that the physical and psychological factors associated with learning theory[14] are capable of producing rather steep concave profiles, like TT and even $T'T'$ in Chart 1, should make one hesitate in relating them to education and other conventional investments. The converse is also true, however: the fact that many investments in human capital in a market economy would produce "the learning

13 See, for example, J. Mincer, "Investment in Human Capital and Personal Income Distribution," *Journal of Political Economy*, August 1958, pp. 287-288.

14 See, e.g., R. Bush and F. Mosteller, *Stochastic Models for Learning*, New York, 1955.

curve" should make one hesitate in relating it to the various factors associated with learning theory.

Another frequent criticism is that many on-the-job investments are really free in that earnings are not reduced at any age. Although this would be formally consistent with my analysis since the rate of return need only be considered infinite (in Chart 1, TT would be nowhere below UU), I suspect that a closer examination of the alleged "facts" would usually reveal a much more conventional situation. For example, if abler employees were put through executive training programs, as is probable, they might earn no less than employees outside the programs but they might earn less than if they had not been in training.[15] Again, the earnings of employees receiving specific training may not be reduced for the reasons presented in Chapter II. Finally, one must have a very poor opinion of the ability of firms to look out for their own interests to believe that infinite rates of return are of great importance.

So much in defense of the approach. To estimate costs empirically still requires a priori knowledge that nothing is invested in activity X. Without such knowledge, only the *difference* between the amounts invested in any two activities with known net earning streams could be estimated from the definitions in equation (28). Were this done for all available streams, the investment in any activity beyond that in the activity with the smallest investment could be determined.[16] The observed minimum investment would not be zero, however, if the rate of return on some initial investment were sufficiently high to attract everyone. A relevant question is, therefore: can the shape of the stream in an activity with zero investment be specified a priori so that the total investment in any activity can be determined?

The statement "nothing is invested in an activity" only means that nothing was invested after the age when information on earnings first became available; investment can have occurred before that age. If, for example, the data begin at age eighteen, some investment in schooling, health, or information surely must have occurred at younger ages. The earning stream of persons who do not invest after age eighteen would have to be considered, at least in part, as a return on the investment before eighteen. Indeed, in the developmental ap-

---

[15] Some indirect evidence is cited by J. Mincer "On-the-Job Training: Costs, Returns, and Some Implications," *Investment in Human Beings*, NBER Special Conference 15, supplement to *Journal of Political Economy*, October 1962, p. 53.

[16] The technique has been applied and developed further by Mincer (*ibid.*).

proach to child-rearing, most if not all of these earnings would be so considered.

The earning stream in an activity with no investment beyond the initial age (activity X) would be flat if the developmental approach were followed and earnings were said to result entirely from earlier investment.[17] The incorporation of learning into the concept of investment in human capital also suggests that earnings profiles would be flat were there no (additional) investment. Finally, the empirical evidence, for what it is worth (see comments in Chapter VII), suggests that earnings profiles in unskilled occupations are quite flat. If the earnings profile in X were flat, the unobserved investment could easily be determined in the usual way once an assumption were made about its rate of return.

The assumption that lifetimes are infinite, although descriptively unrealistic, often yields results that are a close approximation to the truth. For example, I show later (see Chapter VI, section 2) that the average rate of return on college education in the United States would be only slightly raised if people remained in the labor force indefinitely. A finite earning period has, however, a greater effect on the rate of return of investments made at later ages, say, after forty; indeed, it helps explain why schooling and other investments are primarily made at younger ages.

An analysis of finite earning streams can be approached in two ways. One simply applies the concepts developed for infinite streams and says there is disinvestment in human capital when net earnings are above the amount that could be maintained indefinitely. Investment at younger ages would give way to disinvestment at older ages until no human capital remained at death (or retirement). This approach has several important applications and is used in parts of the study (see especially Chapter VII). An alternative that is more useful for some purposes lets the earning period itself influence the definitions of accrued income and cost. The income resulting from an investment during period j would be defined as

$$k_j = \frac{r_j C_j}{1 - (1 + r_j)^{j-n}}, \tag{30}$$

[17] If C measured the cost of investment before the initial age and r its rate of return, $k = rC$ would measure the return per period. If earnings were attributed entirely to this investment, $X_i = k = rC$, where X_i represents earnings at the ith period past the initial age.

where $n + 1$ is the earning period, and the amount invested during j would be defined by

$$C_j = X_j - Y_j + \sum_{k=0}^{k=j-1} \frac{r_k C_k}{1 - (1 + r_k)^{k-n}}. \tag{31}$$

2. The Incentive to Invest

NUMBER OF PERIODS

Economists have long believed that the incentive to expand and improve physical resources depends on the rate of return expected. They have been very reluctant, however, to interpret improvements in the effectiveness and amount of human resources in the same way, namely, as systematic responses or "investments" resulting in good part from the returns expected. In this section and the next one, I try to show that an investment approach to human resources is a powerful and simple tool capable of explaining a wide range of phenomena, including much that has been either ignored or given *ad hoc* interpretations. The discussion covers many topics, starting with the lifespan of activities and ending with a theory of the distribution of earnings.

An increase in the lifespan of an activity would, other things the same, increase the rate of return on the investment made in any period. The influence of lifespan on the rate of return and thus on the incentive to invest is important and takes many forms, a few of which will now be discussed.

The number of periods is clearly affected by mortality and morbidity rates; the lower they are, the longer is the expected lifespan and the larger is the fraction of a lifetime that can be spent at any activity. The major secular decline of these rates in the United States and elsewhere probably increased the rates of return on investment in human capital,[18] thereby encouraging such investment.[19] This con-

[18] I say *probably* because rates of return are adversely affected (via the effects on marginal productivity) by the increase in labor force that would result from a decline in death and sickness. If the adverse effect were sufficiently great, their decline would reduce rates of return on human capital. I am indebted to my wife for emphasizing this point.

[19] The relation between investment in training and length of life is apparently even found in the training of animals, as evidenced by this statement from a book I read to my children: "Working elephants go through a long period of schooling. Training requires about ten years and costs nearly five thousand dollars. In view of the animal's long life of usefulness [they usually live more than sixty years], this is not considered too great an investment" (M. H. Wilson, *Animals of the World*, New York, 1960).

clusion is independent of whether the secular improvement in health itself resulted from investment; if so, the secular increase in rates of return would be part of the return to the investment in health.

A relatively large fraction of younger persons are in school or on-the-job training, change jobs and locations, and add to their knowledge of economic, political, and social opportunities. The main explanation may not be that the young are relatively more interested in learning, able to absorb new ideas, less tied down by family responsibilities, more easily supported by parents, or more flexible about changing their routine and place of living. One need not rely only on life-cycle effects on capabilities, responsibilities, or attitudes as soon as one recognizes that schooling, training, mobility, and the like are ways to invest in human capital and that younger people have a greater incentive to invest because they can collect the return over more years. Indeed, there would be a greater incentive even if age had no effect on capabilities, responsibilities, and attitudes.

The ability to collect returns over more years would give young persons a much greater incentive to invest even if the internal rate of return did not decline much with age. The internal rate can be seriously misleading here, as the following example indicates. If $100 invested at any age yielded $10 a year additional income forever, the rate of return would be 10 per cent at every age, and there would be no special incentive to invest at younger ages if only the rate of return were taken into account. Consider, however, a cohort of persons aged eighteen deciding when to invest. If the rate of return elsewhere were 5 per cent and if they invested immediately, the present value of the gain would be $100. If they waited five years, the present value of the gain, i.e., as of age eighteen, would only be about $78, or 22 per cent less; if they waited ten years, the present value of the gain would be under $50, or less than half. Accordingly, a considerable incentive would exist for everyone to invest immediately rather than waiting. In less extreme examples some persons might wait until older ages, but the number investing would tend to decline rapidly with age even if the rate of return did not.[20]

[20] One clear application of these considerations can be found in studies of migration, where some writers have rejected the importance of the period of returns because migration rates decline strongly with age, at least initially, while rates of return (or some equivalent) decline slowly (see the otherwise fine paper by L. Sjaastad, "The Costs and Returns of Human Migration," *Investment in Human Beings*, pp. 89-90). My analysis suggests, however, that persons with a clear gain from migration

Although the unification of these different kinds of behavior by the investment approach is important evidence in its favor, other evidence is needed. A powerful test can be developed along the following lines.[21] Suppose that investment in human capital raised earnings for p periods only, where p varied between 0 and n. The size of p would be affected by many factors, including the rate of obsolescence since the more rapidly an investment became obsolete the smaller p would be. The advantage in being young would be less the smaller p was, since the effect of age on the rate of return would be positively related to p. For example, if p equaled two years, the rate would be the same at all ages except the two nearest the "retirement" age. If the investment approach were correct, the difference between the amount invested at different ages would be positively correlated with p, which is not surprising since an expenditure with a small p would be less of an "investment" than one with a large p, and arguments based on an investment framework would be less applicable. None of the life-cycle arguments seem to imply any correlation with p, so this provides a powerful test of the importance of the investment approach.

The time spent in any one activity is determined not only by age, mortality, and morbidity but also by the amount of switching between activities. Women spend less time in the labor force than men and, therefore, have less incentive to invest in market skills; tourists spend little time in any one area and have less incentive than residents of the area to invest in knowledge of specific consumption opportunities;[22] temporary migrants to urban areas have less incentive to invest in urban skills than permanent residents; and, as a final example, draftees have less incentive than professional soldiers to invest in purely military skills.

Women, tourists, and the like have to find investments that increase productivity in several activities. A woman wants her investment to be useful both as a housewife and as a participant in the labor force,

---

have a strong incentive to migrate early and not wait even a few years. Since the persons remaining presumably have either no incentive or little incentive to migrate, it is not surprising that their migration rates should be much lower than that of all persons.

21 This test was suggested by George Stigler's discussion of the effect of different autocorrelation patterns on the incentive to invest in information (see "The Economics of Information," *Journal of Political Economy*, June 1961, and "Information in the Labor Market" in *Investment in Human Beings*, pp. 94-105).

22 This example is from Stigler, "The Economics of Information," *Journal of Political Economy*, June 1961.

or a frequent traveler wants to be knowledgeable in many environments. Such investments would be less readily available than more specialized ones—after all, an investment increasing productivity in two activities also increases it in either one alone, extreme complementarity aside, while the converse does not hold; specialists, therefore, have greater incentive to invest in themselves than others do.

Specialization in an activity would be discouraged if the market were very limited; thus the incentive to specialize and to invest in oneself would increase as the extent of the market increased. Workers would be more skilled the larger the market, not only because "practice makes perfect," which is so often stressed in discussions of the division of labor,[23] but also because a larger market would *induce* a greater investment in skills.[24] Put differently, the usual analysis of the division of labor stresses that efficiency, and thus wage rates, would be greater the larger the market, and ignores the potential earnings period in any activity, while mine stresses that this period, and thus the incentive to *become* more "efficient," would be directly related to market size. Surprisingly little attention has been paid to the latter, that is, to the influence of market size on the incentive to invest in skills.

WAGE DIFFERENTIALS AND SECULAR CHANGES

According to equation (30), the internal rate of return depends on the ratio of the return per unit of time to investment costs. A change in the return and costs by the same percentage would not change the internal rate, while a greater percentage change in the return would change the internal rate in the same direction. The return is measured by the absolute income gain, or by the absolute income difference between persons differing only in the amount of their investment. Note that absolute, not relative, income differences determine the return and the internal rate.

Occupational and educational wage differentials are sometimes

[23] See, for example, A. Marshall, *Principles of Economics*, New York, 1949, Bk. IV, Chap. ix.
[24] If "practice makes perfect" means that age-earnings profiles slope upward, then according to my approach it must be treated along with other kinds of learning as a way of investing in human capital. The above distinction between the effect of an increase in the market on practice and on the incentive to invest would then simply be that the incentive to invest in human capital is increased even aside from the effect of practice on earnings.

measured by relative, sometimes by absolute, wage differences,[25] although no one has adequately discussed their relative merits. Since marginal productivity analysis relates the derived demand for any class of workers to the ratio of their wages to those of other inputs,[26] wage ratios are more appropriate in understanding forces determining demand. They are not, however, the best measure of forces determining supply, for the return on investment in skills and other knowledge is determined by absolute wage differences. Therefore neither wage ratios nor wage differences are uniformly the best measure, ratios being more appropriate in demand studies and differences in supply studies.

The importance of distinguishing between wage ratios and differences, and the confusion resulting from the practice of using ratios to measure supply as well as demand forces, can be illustrated by considering the effects of technological progress. If progress were uniform in all industries and neutral with respect to all factors, and if there were constant costs, initially all wages would rise by the same proportion and the prices of all goods, including the output of industries supplying the investment in human capital,[27] would be unchanged. Since wage ratios would be unchanged, firms would have no incentive initially to alter their factor proportions. Wage differences, on the other hand, would rise at the same rate as wages, and since investment costs would be unchanged, there would be an incentive to invest more in human capital, and thus to increase the relative supply of skilled persons. The increased supply would in turn reduce the rate of increase of wage differences and produce an absolute narrowing of wage ratios.

In the United States during much of the last eighty years, a narrow-

25 See A. M. Ross and W. Goldner, "Forces Affecting the Interindustry Wage Structure," *Quarterly Journal of Economics,* May 1950; P. H. Bell, "Cyclical Variations and Trend in Occupational Wage Differentials in American Industry since 1914," *Review of Economics and Statistics,* November 1951; F. Meyers and R. L. Bowlby, "The Interindustry Wage Structure and Productivity," *Industrial and Labor Relations Review,* October 1953; G. Stigler and D. Blank, *The Demand and Supply of Scientific Personnel,* New York, NBER, 1957, Table 11; P. Keat, "Long-Run Changes in Occupational Wage Structure, 1900-1956," *Journal of Political Economy,* December 1960.

26 Thus the elasticity of substitution is usually defined as the percentage change in the ratio of quantities employed per 1 per cent change in the ratio of wages.

27 Some persons have argued that only direct investment costs would be unchanged, indirect costs or foregone earnings rising along with wages. Neutral progress implies, however, the same increase in the productivity of a student's time as in his teacher's time or in the use of raw materials, so even foregone earnings would not change.

ing of wage ratios has gone hand in hand with an increasing relative supply of skill, an association that is usually said to result from the effect of an autonomous increase in the supply of skills—brought about by the spread of free education or the rise in incomes—on the return to skill, as measured by wage ratios. An alternative interpretation suggested by the analysis here is that the spread of education and the increased investment in other kinds of human capital were in large part *induced* by technological progress (and perhaps other changes) through the effect on the rate of return, as measured by wage differences and costs. Clearly a secular decline in wage ratios would not be inconsistent with a secular increase in real wage differences if average wages were rising, and, indeed, one important body of data on wages shows a decline in ratios and an even stronger rise in differences.[28]

The interpretation based on autonomous supply shifts has been favored partly because a decline in wage ratios has erroneously been taken as evidence of a decline in the return to skill. While a decision ultimately can be based only on a detailed re-examination of the evidence,[29] the induced approach can be made more plausible by considering trends in physical capital. Economists have been aware that the rate of return on capital could be rising or at least not falling while the ratio of the "rental" price of capital to wages was falling. Consequently, although the rental price of capital declined relative to wages over time, the large secular increase in the amount of physical capital per man-hour is not usually considered autonomous, but rather induced by technological and other developments that, at least temporarily, raised the return. A common explanation based on the

[28] Keat's data for 1906 and 1953 in the United States show both an average annual decline of 0.8 per cent in the coefficient of variation of wages and an average annual rise of 1.2 per cent in the real standard deviation. The decline in the coefficient of variation was shown in his study (*ibid.*); I computed the change in the real standard deviation from data made available to me by Keat.

[29] For those believing that the qualitative evidence overwhelmingly indicates a continuous secular decline in rates of return on human capital, I reproduce Adam Smith's statement on earnings in some professions. "The lottery of the law, therefore, is very far from being a perfectly fair lottery; and that, as well as many other liberal and honourable professions, is, in point of pecuniary gain, evidently under-recompensed" (*The Wealth of Nations*, Modern Library edition, New York, 1937, p. 106). Since economists tend to believe that law and most other liberal professions are now overcompensated relative to nonprofessional work "in point of pecuniary gain," the return to professional work could not have declined continuously if Smith's observations were accurate.

effects of economic progress may, then, account for the increase in both human and physical capital.[30]

RISK AND LIQUIDITY

An informed, rational person would invest only if the expected rate of return were greater than the sum of the interest rate on riskless assets and the liquidity and risk premiums associated with the investment. Not much need be said about the "pure" interest rate, but a few words are in order on risk and liquidity. Since human capital is a very illiquid asset—it cannot be sold and is rather poor collateral on loans—a positive liquidity premium, perhaps a sizable one, would be associated with such capital.

The actual return on human capital varies around the expected return because of uncertainty about several factors. There has always been considerable uncertainty about the length of life, one important determinant of the return. People are also uncertain about their ability, especially younger persons who do most of the investing. In addition, there is uncertainty about the return to a person of given age and ability because of numerous events that are not predictable. The long time required to collect the return on an investment in human capital reduces the knowledge available, for knowledge required is about the environment when the return is to be received, and the longer the average period between investment and return, the less such knowledge is available.

Informed observation as well as calculations I have made suggest that there is much uncertainty about the return to human capital.[31] The response to uncertainty is determined by its amount and nature and by tastes or attitudes. Many have argued that attitudes of investors in human capital are very different from those of investors in

---

[30] Some quantitative evidence for the United States is discussed in Chapter VI, section 2.

[31] For example, Marshall said: "Not much less than a generation elapses between the choice by parents of a skilled trade for one of their children, and his reaping the full results of their choice. And meanwhile the character of the trade may have been almost revolutionized by changes, on which some probably threw long shadows before them, but others were such as could not have been foreseen even by the shrewdest persons and those best acquainted with the circumstances of the trade" and "the circumstances by which the earnings are determined are less capable of being foreseen [than those for machinery]" (*Principles of Economics*, p. 571). In section 4 of Chapter IV some quantitative estimates of the uncertainty in the return to education are presented.

physical capital because the former tend to be younger,[32] and young persons are supposed to be especially prone to overestimate their ability and chance of good fortune.[33] Were this view correct, a human investment which promised a large return to exceptionally able or lucky persons would be more attractive than a similar physical investment. However, a "life-cycle" explanation of attitudes toward risk may be no more valid or necessary than life-cycle explanations of why investors in human capital are relatively young (discussed above). Indeed, an alternative explanation of reactions to large gains has already appeared.[34]

CAPITAL MARKETS AND KNOWLEDGE

If investment decisions responded only to earning prospects, adjusted for risk and liquidity, the adjusted marginal rate of return would be the same on all investments. The rate of return on education, training, migration, health, and other human capital is supposed to be higher than on nonhuman capital, however, because of financing difficulties and inadequate knowledge of opportunities. These will now be discussed briefly.

Economists have long emphasized that it is difficult to borrow funds to invest in human capital because such capital cannot be offered as collateral, and courts have frowned on contracts which even indirectly suggest involuntary servitude. This argument has been explicitly used to explain the "apparent" underinvestment in education and training and also, although somewhat less explicitly, underinvestment in health, migration, and other human capital. The importance attached to capital market difficulties can be determined not only from the discussions of investment but also from the discussions of consumption. Young persons would consume relatively little, productivity and wages might be related, and some other consumption patterns would follow only if it were difficult to capitalize future earning power. In-

---

[32] Note that our argument above implied that investors in human capital would be younger.

[33] Smith said: "The contempt of risk and the presumptuous hope of success, are in no period of life more active than at the age at which young people choose their professions" (*Wealth of Nations*, p. 109). Marshall said that "young men of an adventurous disposition are more attracted by the prospects of a great success than they are deterred by the fear of failure" (*Principles of Economics*, p. 554).

[34] See M. Friedman and L. J. Savage, "The Utility Analysis of Choices Involving Risks," reprinted in *Readings in Price Theory*, G. J. Stigler and K. Boulding, eds., Chicago, 1952.

deed, unless capital limitations applied to consumption as well as investment, the latter could be indirectly financed with "consumption" loans.[35]

Some other implications of capital market difficulties can also be mentioned:

1. Since large expenditures would be more difficult to finance, investment in, say, a college education would be more affected than in, say, short-term migration.

2. Internal financing would be common, and consequently wealthier families would tend to invest more than poorer ones.

3. Since employees' specific skills are part of the intangible assets or good will of firms and can be offered as collateral along with tangible assets, capital would be more readily available for specific than for general investments.

4. Some persons have argued that opportunity costs (foregone earnings) are more readily financed than direct costs because they require only to do "without," while the latter require outlays. Although superficially plausible, this view can easily be shown to be wrong: opportunity and direct costs can be financed equally readily, given the state of the capital market. If total investment costs were $800, potential earnings $1,000, and if all costs were foregone earnings, investors would have $200 of earnings to spend; if all were direct costs, they would initially have $1,000 to spend, but just $200 would remain after paying "tuition," so their *net* position would be exactly the same as before. The example can be readily generalized and the obvious inference is that indirect and direct investment costs are equivalent in imperfect as well as perfect capital markets.

While it is undeniably difficult to use the capital market to finance investments in human capital, there is some reason to doubt whether otherwise equivalent investments in physical capital can be financed much more easily. Consider an eighteen-year-old who wants to invest a given amount in equipment for a firm he is starting rather than in a college education. What is his chance of borrowing the whole amount at a "moderate" interest rate? Very slight, I believe, since he would be untried and have a high debt-equity ratio; moreover, the

---

[35] A person with an income of X and investment costs of Y (Y < X) could either use X for consumption and receive an *investment loan* of Y, or use X — Y for consumption, Y for investment, and receive a *consumption loan* of Y. He ends up with the same consumption and investment in both cases, the only difference being in the names attached to the loans.

collateral provided by his equipment would probably be very imperfect. He, too, would either have to borrow at high interest rates or
self-finance. Although the difficulties of financing investments in
human capital have usually been related to special properties of
human capital, in large measure they also seem to beset comparable
investments in physical capital.

A recurring theme is that young persons are especially prone to be
ignorant of their abilities and of the investment opportunities available. If so, investors in human capital, being younger, would be less
aware of opportunities and thus more likely to err than investors in
tangible capital. I suggested earlier that investors in human capital
are younger partly because of the cost in postponing their investment
to older ages. The desire to acquire additional knowledge about the
return and about alternatives provides an incentive to postpone any
risky investment, but since an investment in human capital is more
costly to postpone, it would be made earlier and presumably with less
knowledge than comparable nonhuman investments. Therefore, investors in human capital may not have less knowledge *because* of their
age; rather both might be a *joint* product of the incentive not to
delay investing.

The eighteen-year-old in our example who could not finance a pur-
chase of machinery might, without too much cost, postpone the investment for a number of years until his reputation and equity were
sufficient to provide the "personal" collateral required to borrow
funds. Financing may prove a more formidable obstacle to investors
in human capital because they cannot postpone their investment so
readily. Perhaps this accounts for the tendency of economists to stress
capital market imperfections when discussing investments in human
capital.

3. Some Effects of Human Capital

EXAMPLES

Differences in earnings among persons, areas, or time periods are
usually said to result from differences in physical capital, technological knowledge, ability, or institutions (such as unionization or social-
ized production). The previous discussion indicates, however, that
investment in human capital also has an important effect on observed
earnings because earnings tend to be net of investment costs and gross
of investment returns. Indeed, an appreciation of the direct and in-

direct importance of human capital appears to resolve many otherwise puzzling empirical findings about earnings. Consider the following examples:

1. Almost all studies show that age-earnings profiles tend to be steeper among more skilled and educated persons. I argued earlier (Chapter II, section 1) that on-the-job training would steepen age-earnings profiles, and the analysis of section 1 of this chapter generalizes the argument to all human capital. For since observed earnings are gross of returns and net of costs, investment in human capital at younger ages would reduce observed earnings then and raise them at older ages, thus steepening the age-earnings profile.[36] Likewise, investment in human capital would make the profile more concave.[37]

2. In recent years students of international trade theory have been somewhat shaken by findings that the United States, said to have a relative scarcity of labor and an abundance of capital, apparently exports relatively labor-intensive commodities and imports relatively capital-intensive commodities. For example, one study found that

[36] According to eq. (28) earnings at age j can be approximated by

$$\Upsilon_j = X_j + \sum_{k=0}^{k=j-1} r_k C_k - C_j,$$

where X_j are earnings at j of persons who have not invested in themselves, C_k is the investment at age k, and r_k is its rate of return. The rate of increase in earnings would be at least as steep in Y as in X at each age and not only from "younger" to "older" ages if and only if

$$\frac{\Delta \Upsilon_j}{\Delta j} \geq \frac{\Delta X_j}{\Delta j},$$

or

$$r_j C_j \geq \frac{\Delta C_j}{\Delta j}.$$

This condition is usually satisfied since $r_j C_j \geq 0$ and the amount invested tends to decline with age.

[37] Following the notation of the previous footnote, Y would be more concave than X if and only if

$$\Delta \left(\frac{\Delta \Upsilon_j}{\Delta j}\right) - \Delta \left(\frac{\Delta X_j}{\Delta j}\right) = \Delta \left(\frac{r_j C_j}{\Delta j}\right) - \Delta \left(\frac{\Delta C_j}{\Delta j}\right) < 0.$$

The first term on the right is certain to be negative, at least eventually, because both r_j and C_j would eventually decline, while the second term would be positive because C_j would eventually decline at a decreasing rate. Consequently, the inequality would tend to hold and the earnings profile in Y would be more concave than that in X.

export industries pay higher wages than import-competing ones.[38]

An interpretation consistent with the Ohlin-Heckscher emphasis on the relative abundance of different factors argues that the United States has an even more (relatively) abundant supply of human than of physical capital. An increase in human capital would, however, show up as an apparent increase in labor intensity since earnings are gross of the return on such capital. Thus export industries might pay higher wages than import-competing ones primarily because they employ more skilled or healthier workers.[39]

3. Several recent studies have tried to estimate empirically the elasticity of substitution between capital and labor. Usually a ratio of the input of physical capital (or output) to the input of labor is regressed on the wage rate in different areas or time periods, the regression coefficient being an estimate of the elasticity of substitution.[40] Countries, states, or time periods that have relatively high wages and inputs of physical capital also tend to have much human capital. Just as a correlation between wages, physical capital, and human capital seems to obscure the relationship between relative factor supplies and commodity prices, so it obscures the relationship between relative factor supplies and factor prices. For if wages were high primarily because of human capital, a regression of the relative amount of physical capital on wages could give a seriously biased picture of the effect on wages of factor proportions.[41]

[38] See I. Kravis, "Wages and Foreign Trade," *Review of Economics and Statistics,* February 1956.

[39] This kind of interpretation has been put forward by many writers; see, for example, the discussion in W. Leontief, "Factor Proportions and the Structure of American Trade: Further Theoretical and Empirical Analysis," *Review of Economics and Statistics,* November 1956.

[40] Interstate estimates for several industries can be found in J. Minasian, "Elasticities of Substitution and Constant-Output Demand Curves for Labor," *Journal of Political Economy,* June 1961, pp. 261-270; intercountry estimates in Kenneth Arrow, Hollis B. Chenery, Bagicha Minhas, and Robert M. Solow, "Capital-Labor Substitution and Economic Efficiency," *Review of Economics and Statistics,* August 1961; as yet unpublished studies by Philip Nelson and Robert Solow contain both interstate and time-series estimates.

[41] Minasian's argument (in his article cited above, p. 264) that interstate variations in skill level necessarily bias his estimates toward unity is actually correct only if skill is a perfect substitute for "labor." (In correspondence Minasian stated that he intended to make this condition explicit.) If, on the other hand, human and physical capital were perfect substitutes, I have shown (in an unpublished memorandum) that the estimates would always have a downward bias, regardless of the true substitution between labor and capital. Perhaps the most reasonable assumption would be that physical capital is more complementary with human capital than with labor; I have not, however, been able generally to determine the direction of bias in this case.

4. A secular increase in average earnings has usually been said to result from increases in technological knowledge and physical capital per earner. The average earner, in effect, is supposed to benefit indirectly from activities by entrepreneurs, investors, and others. Another explanation put forward in recent years argues that earnings can rise because of direct investment in earners.[42] Instead of only benefiting from activities by others, the average earner is made a prime mover of development through the investment in himself.[43]

ABILITY AND THE DISTRIBUTION OF EARNINGS

An emphasis on human capital not only helps explain differences in earnings over time and among areas but also among persons or families within an area. This application will be discussed in greater detail than the others because a link is provided between earnings, ability, and the incentive to invest in human capital.

Economists have long been aware that conventional measures of ability—intelligence tests or aptitude scores, school grades, and personality tests—while undoubtedly relevant at times, do not reliably measure the talents required to succeed in the economic sphere. The latter consists of particular kinds of personality, persistence, and intelligence. Accordingly, some writers have gone to the opposite extreme and argued that the only relevant way to measure economic talent is by results, or by earnings themselves.[44] Persons with higher earnings would simply have more ability than others, and a skewed distribution of earnings would imply a skewed distribution of abilities. This approach goes too far, however, in the opposite direction. The main reason for relating ability to earning is to distinguish its effects from

---

D. O'Neill has recently finished a dissertation at Columbia University in which estimates of human capital are explicitly incorporated into the cross-sectional regressions.

42 The major figure here is T. W. Schultz. Of his many articles, see especially "Education and Economic Growth" in *Social Forces Influencing American Education,* Sixtieth Yearbook of the National Society for the Study of Education, Chicago, 1961, Part II, Chap. 3.

43 One caveat is called for, however. Since observed earnings are not only gross of the return from investments in human capital but also are net of some costs, an increased investment in human capital would both raise and reduce earnings. Although average earnings would tend to increase as long as the rate of return was positive, the increase would be less than if the cost of human capital, like that of physical capital, was not deducted from national income.

44 Let me state again that the word "earnings" stands for real earnings, or the sum of monetary earnings and the monetary equivalent of psychic earnings.

differences in education, training, health, and other such factors, and a definition equating ability and earnings *ipso facto* precludes such a distinction. Nevertheless, results are very relevant and should not be ignored.

A compromise might be reached through defining ability by earnings only when several variables have been held constant. Since the public is very concerned about separating ability from education, on-the-job training, health, and other human capital, the amount invested in such capital would have to be held constant. Although a full analysis would also hold discrimination, nepotism, luck, and several other factors constant, a reasonable first approximation would say that if two persons have the same investment in human capital, the one who earns more is demonstrating greater economic talent.

Since observed earnings are gross of the return on human capital, they are affected by changes in the amount and rate of return. Indeed, it has been shown that, after the investment period, earnings (Y) can be simply approximated by

$$Y = X + rC, \tag{32}$$

where C measures total investment costs, r the average rate of return, and X earnings when there is no investment in human capital. If the distribution of X is ignored for now, Y would depend only on r when C was held constant, so "ability" would be measured by the average rate of return on human capital.[45]

In most capital markets the amount invested is not the same for everyone nor rigidly fixed for any given person, but depends in part on the rate of return. Persons receiving a high marginal rate of return would have an incentive to invest more than others.[46] Since marginal and average rates are presumably positively correlated[47] and since

---

[45] Since r is a function of C, Y would indirectly as well as directly depend on C, and therefore the distribution of ability would depend on the amount of human capital. Some persons might rank high in earnings and thus high in ability if everyone were unskilled, and quite low if education and other training were widespread.

[46] In addition, they would find it easier to invest if the marginal return and the resources of parents and other relatives were positively correlated.

[47] According to a well-known formula,

$$r_m = r_a \left(1 + \frac{1}{e_a} \right),$$

where r_m is the marginal rate of return, r_a the average rate, and e_a the elasticity of the average rate with respect to the amount invested. The rates r_m and r_a would be positively correlated unless r_a and $1/e_a$ were sufficiently negatively correlated.

ability is measured by the average rate, one can say that abler persons would invest more than others. The end result would be a positive correlation between ability and the investment in human capital,[48] a correlation with several important implications.

One is that the tendency for abler persons to migrate, continue their education,[49] and generally invest more in themselves can be explained without recourse to an assumption that noneconomic forces or demand conditions favor them at higher investment levels. A second implication is that the separation of "nature from nurture" or ability from education and other environmental factors is apt to be difficult, for high earnings would tend to signify both more ability and a better environment. Thus the earnings differential between college and high-school graduates does not measure the effect of college alone since college graduates are abler and would earn more even without the additional education. Or reliable estimates of the income elasticity of demand for children have been difficult to obtain because higher-income families also invest more in contraceptive knowledge.[50]

The main implication, however, is in personal income distribution. At least ever since the time of Pigou economists have tried to reconcile the strong skewness in the distribution of earnings and other income with a presumed symmetrical distribution of abilities.[51] Pigou's main suggestion—that property income is not symmetrically distributed—does not directly help explain the skewness in earnings. Subsequent attempts have largely concentrated on developing *ad hoc* random and other probabilistic mechanisms that have little relation to the mainstream of economic thought.[52] The approach presented here, however,

[48] This kind of argument is not new; Marshall argued that business ability and the ownership of physical capital would be positively correlated: "[economic] forces . . . bring about the result that there is a far more close correspondence between the ability of business men and the size of the businesses which they own than at first sight would appear probable" (*Principles of Economics*, p. 312).

[49] The first is frequently alleged (see, for example, *ibid.*, p. 199). Evidence on the second is discussed in Chapter IV, section 2.

[50] See my "An Economic Analysis of Fertility" in *Demographic and Economic Change in Developed Countries*, Special Conference 11, Princeton for NBER, 1960.

[51] See A. C. Pigou, *The Economics of Welfare*, 4th ed., London, 1950, Part IV, Chap. ii.

[52] A sophisticated example can be found in B. Mandelbrot, "The Pareto-Lévy Law and the Distribution of Income," *International Economic Review*, May 1960. In a recent paper, however, Mandelbrot has brought in maximizing behavior (see "Paretian Distributions and Income Maximization," *Quarterly Journal of Economics*, February 1962).

offers an explanation that is not only consistent with economic analysis but actually relies on one of its fundamental tenets, namely, that the amount invested is a function of the rate of return expected. In conjunction with the effect of human capital on earnings, this tenet can explain several well-known properties of earnings distributions.

By definition, the distribution of earnings would be exactly the same as the distribution of ability if everyone invested the same amount in human capital; in particular, if ability were symmetrically distributed, earnings would also be. Equation (32) shows that the distribution of earnings would be exactly the same as the distribution of investment if all persons were equally able; again, if investment were symmetrically distributed, earnings would also be.[53] If ability and investment both varied, earnings would tend to be skewed even when ability and investment were not, but the skewness would be small as long as the amount invested were statistically independent of ability.[54]

It has been shown, however, that abler persons would tend to invest

---

[53] Jacob Mincer ("Investment in Human Capital and Personal Income Distribution," *Journal of Political Economy,* August 1958) concluded that a symmetrical distribution of investment in education implies a skewed distribution of earnings because he defines educational investment by school years rather than costs. If Mincer is followed in assuming that everyone was equally able, that schooling was the only investment, and that the cost of the nth year of schooling equaled the earnings of persons with $n - 1$ years of schooling, then, say, a normal distribution of schooling can be shown to imply a long-normal distribution of school costs and thus a log-normal distribution of earnings.

The difference between the earnings of persons with $n - 1$ and n years of schooling would be $k_n = Y_n - Y_{n-1} = r_n C_n$. Since r_n is assumed to equal r for all n, and $C_n = Y_{n-1}$, this equation becomes $Y_n = (1 + r) Y_{n-1}$, and therefore

$$C_1 = Y_0$$
$$C_2 = Y_1 = Y_0 (1 + r)$$
$$C_3 = Y_2 = Y_1 (1 + r) = Y_0 (1 + r)^2$$
$$C_n = Y_{n-1} = \ldots = Y_0 (1 + r)^{n-1} \quad ,$$

or the cost of each additional year of schooling increases at a constant *rate*. Since total costs have the same distribution as $(1 + r)^n$, a symmetrical, say, a normal, distribution of school years, n, implies a log-normal distribution of costs and hence by eq. (32) a log-normal distribution of earnings. I am indebted to Mincer for a helpful discussion of the comparison and especially for the stimulation provided by his pioneering work. Incidentally, his article and the dissertation on which it is based cover a much broader area than has been indicated here.

[54] For example, C. C. Craig has shown that the product of two independent normal distributions is only slightly skewed (see his "On the Frequency Function of XY," *Annals of Mathematical Statistics,* March 1936, p. 3).

more than others, so ability and investment would be positively correlated, perhaps quite strongly. Now the product of two symmetrical
distributions is more positively skewed the higher the positive correlation between them, and might be quite skewed.[55] The economic
incentive given abler persons to invest relatively large amounts in
themselves does seem capable, therefore, of reconciling a strong positive skewness in earnings with a presumed symmetrical distribution of
abilities.

Variations in X help explain an important difference among skill
categories in the degree of skewness. The smaller the fraction of total
earnings resulting from investment in human capital—the smaller rC
relative to X—the more the distribution of earnings would be dominated by the distribution of X. Higher-skill categories have a greater
average investment in human capital and thus presumably a larger
rC relative to X. The distribution of "unskilled ability," X, would,
therefore, tend to dominate the distribution of earnings in relatively
unskilled categories while the distribution of a product of ability and
the amount invested, rC, would dominate in skilled categories. Hence
if abilities were symmetrically distributed, earnings would tend to be
more symmetrically distributed among the unskilled than among the
skilled.[56]

Equation (32) holds only when investment costs are small, which
tends to be true at later ages, say, after age 35. Net earnings at earlier
ages would be given by

$$Y_j = X_j + \sum_0^{j-1} r_i C_i + (-C_j), \qquad (33)$$

where j refers to the current year and i to previous years, C_i measures
the investment cost of age i, C_j current costs, and r_i the rate of return
on C_j. The distribution of $-C_j$ would be an important determinant

---

[55] Craig (*ibid.*, pp. 9-10) showed that the product of two normal distributions would
be more positively skewed the higher the positive correlation between them, and that
the skewness would be considerable with high correlations.

[56] As noted earlier, X does not really represent earnings when there is no investment in human capital, but only earnings when there is no investment after the initial
age (be it 14, 25, or 6). Indeed, the developmental approach to child-rearing argues
that earnings would be close to zero if there were no investment at all in human
capital. The distribution of X, therefore, would be at least partly determined by the
distribution of investment before the initial age, and if it and ability were positively
correlated, X might be positively skewed, even though ability was not.

of the distribution of Y_j since investment is large at these ages. Hence the analysis would predict a smaller (positive) skewness at younger than at older ages partly because X would be more important relative to $\Sigma r_i C_i$ at younger ages and partly because the presumed negative correlation between $-C_j$ and $\displaystyle\sum_0^{j-1} r_i C_i$ would counteract the positive correlation between r_i and C_i.

A simple analysis of the incentive to invest in human capital seems capable of explaining, therefore, not only why the over-all distribution of earnings is more skewed than the distribution of abilities, but also why earnings are more skewed among older and skilled persons than among younger and less skilled ones. The renewed interest in investment in human capital may provide the means of bringing the theory of personal income distribution back into economics.

PART TWO

EMPIRICAL ANALYSIS

"An investment in knowledge
pays the best interest."

Benjamin Franklin, *Poor Richard's Almanack*

CHAPTER IV

Rates of Return from College Education

VIRTUALLY all the implications developed in Part One, from income distributions to unemployment, are based on the effect of investment in human capital on earnings and productivity. Consequently, the significance of that analysis can be determined most directly through an empirical examination of the relation between earnings or productivity and human capital. This will be done in the next three chapters for a number of time periods and demographic groups in the United States.

Although an investigation of many kinds of human capital would be illuminating, the absence of readily available data makes it necessary to concentrate primarily on formal education. Fortunately, education is of considerable interest in its own right and a matter of much current concern: laymen, policy-makers, and researchers are all worrying about the role of education in promoting economic and cultural progress, and about ways to improve the educational process. Quantitative evidence on the economic effects of education would add an important dimension to these discussions because all too often they have been based on grossly inaccurate economic notions.

This chapter and the following one estimate rates of return on college education in the United States during recent years, and Chapter VI covers high-school education and earlier years. Rates of return provide the most convenient and complete summary of the economic effects of education and, therefore, can be used to answer a variety of questions, such as the following:

1. Do relatively few female, nonwhite, and rural high-school graduates attend college primarily because of relatively low rates of return, or because of financial difficulties, discrimination, and still other factors?

2. Are private rates of return higher on education than on physical capital and, if so, is the explanation to be found in risk, ignorance of effects, nonpecuniary factors, or imperfections in the capital market? Has the large subsidy to education reduced its social rate of return below that on other capital, or has the subsidy been an inadequate response to a very large discrepancy between social and private returns from education?

3. Do more intelligent persons receive higher rates of return from education than others?

4. Has the large secular growth in education caused a decline in returns from education, or has the growth itself been induced by an increase in returns?

The materials analyzed in these chapters shed appreciable light on these and other questions, although, of course, definitive answers are not provided.

This chapter presents estimates of rates of return to urban white males who graduated from college after 1939, estimates for college drop-outs, and estimates for college-educated women, nonwhites, and rural persons. Considerable attention is paid to determining the dispersion in rates of return on college education.

1. Money Rates of Return to White Male College Graduates

RETURNS IN 1939

The effect of education on income could easily be determined if information were available on the income of units differing only in education, for then differences in income could be attributed solely to differences in education. These could be geographical units, as countries or states; time units, as the United States today and, say, fifty years ago; or individuals, as college and high-school graduates in the United States. Unfortunately, units differing in education also tend to differ in other factors that influence incomes. For example, higher-income geographical units also tend to have more physical capital per person, while college graduates tend to be abler than high-school graduates. In other words, the raw information has to be standardized for other factors in order to isolate the effect of education. A few attempts have been made to standardize the information on geographical units, and although interesting qualitative results have emerged, only a limited quantitative analysis has been possible.[1] I decided to exploit the extensive data available for the United States since the 1930's on the earnings and incomes of persons with different amounts of education because they seemed most capable of yielding quantitative, although admittedly rough, estimates of rates of return on education.

TABLE 1

ACTUAL EARNING DIFFERENTIALS BETWEEN URBAN, NATIVE-WHITE, MALE COLLEGE AND HIGH-SCHOOL GRADUATES IN 1939 AT VARIOUS AGES

Age	Percentage (1)	Absolute (2)
23-24	4	51
25-29	29	455
30-34	47	949
35-44	56	1,449
45-54	59	1,684
55-64	53	1,386
18-19	-108	-557
20-21	-95	-805
22	-46	-487

Source: Basic data from *1940 Census of Population, Educational Attainment by Economic Characteristics and Marital Status*, Bureau of the Census, Washington, 1947, Table 29, p. 148. M. Zeman estimated mean incomes at various age and education classes from the Census data (see his "A Quantitative Analysis of White-Non-White Income Differentials in the United States in 1939," unpublished Ph.D. dissertation, University of Chicago, 1955). These data were adjusted for the underreporting of professional earnings (see my Table A-6), the underreporting of wages and salaries (see Table A-4), and unemployment (see Table A-5). Cost estimates in the bottom half of the table were obtained by the methods discussed in Appendix A.

The national data on the incomes of persons at different educational levels provided by the 1940 and 1950 Censuses can be supplemented during the 1950's with smaller surveys. Table 1 shows absolute and percentage differences in mean earnings during 1939 at various age classes between urban, native-white, male college and high-school graduates. Average earnings computed from the 1940 Census were uniformly adjusted upward by 10 per cent because of the under-estimation of wages and salaries in the Census data. They were also

[1] One recent exception is a study by Zvi Griliches of the effect of education on agricultural output using counties as the unit of analysis (see his "The Sources of Measured Productivity Growth: United States Agriculture, 1940-60," *Journal of Political Economy*, August 1963, pp. 331-336).

corrected for the abnormally large unemployment in 1939 so that the data could reflect a more normal economic situation.[2] The adjustment for underestimation raises absolute earning differentials but not percentage ones, while the adjustment for unemployment lowers percentage differentials but does not change absolute ones very much. Since only persons with at least $1 of wages or salaries and less than $50 of other income are covered in the 1940 Census, independent professionals and many other persons were excluded. In order to expand the coverage, the earnings of college graduates were considered to be a weighted average at each age of the earnings of college graduates given by the Census and of independent doctors, lawyers, and dentists given elsewhere, the weights being the number of persons in each group. Both the percentage and absolute differences in columns 1 and 2 of Table 1 are substantial and rise with age, averaging about $1,100 (in 1939 dollars) and 45 per cent, respectively, and rising from $450 and 30 per cent at about age 27 to $1,700 and 60 per cent at about age 50.

Since Table 1 gives the income gains of surviving members of different cohorts, one way to relate costs and returns would be to compare these gains with the college costs of the different cohorts. Another, and for my purposes easier, way would be to compare the costs and returns of a given cohort as it ages over time. Since these data are not directly available, the returns to different cohorts as of the moment in time have to be converted into returns to a given cohort aging over time.

The average earnings of a cohort at any age is a weighted average of the earnings of survivors and of those dying earlier. Obviously the latter earn nothing after they die, so the weighted average can be computed simply by multiplying the earnings of survivors by the fraction surviving. Accordingly, the average earnings in 1939 of different cohorts were mutiplied by life table survivorship rates[3] to help convert them into earnings at different ages of a single cohort. Since the same rates were used for high-school and college graduates (although a slightly higher rate should have been used for the latter),

---

[2] A detailed discussion of these and other adjustments can be found in Appendix A.
[3] They should also be multiplied by labor force participation rates because the 1940 Census only includes persons with at least a dollar of earnings in 1939. Experiments on the 1950 Census data indicate, however, that this adjustment has only a slight effect on the results.

percentage earnings differentials were unaffected while absolute ones were lowered, especially at older ages.

The secular growth in real earnings per capita would usually enable the cohort of persons graduating from high school or college in any year to earn more at each age than was earned in that year by persons who had graduated earlier. Earnings received in 1939 have to be adjusted upward, therefore, if they are to represent the earnings of cohorts graduating in 1939. Only part of the substantial rate of growth since 1939 in earnings per capita can be used in the adjustment, however, because much of the growth in earnings resulted from the increase in education itself. Moreover, earnings did not grow at the same rate in all age and education categories. Not being able to make an exhaustive study, I simply assumed that if $d(t)$ were the differential observed in 1939 between cohorts graduating from college and high school t years earlier, the differential t years later for cohorts who had graduated in 1939 would be $d(t)(1 + g)^t$, where g is the annual rate of growth in the differential. The most plausible value for g seems to be about .0125, although results are also presented for $g = 0$ and $g = .02$.[4]

Cross-sectional and cohort earnings also differ in several other respects. For example, the former are much more affected by business cycles, and, consequently, as already mentioned, the 1939 data had to be adjusted for the depressed economic conditions at that time. An interesting difference can be found in the adjustment for income tax payments required to convert before-tax returns into private returns. In 1939 tax rates were low and so only a minor adjustment need be made to incomes received at that time. A much more substantial adjustment, however, has to be made to the incomes of cohorts graduating in 1939 because they received the bulk of their incomes in the 1940's and later, and taxes have risen substantially during these years. Accordingly, two alternative adjustments have been made: one is simply based on the 1939 tax rates, while the other utilizes the much higher rates prevailing in 1949 to approximate the effects of the different tax rates in the 1940's, 1950's, and 1960's.

4 According to E. Denison, national income per capita has grown at a rate of 1.7 per cent per annum from 1929 to 1957 and about 25 per cent of this was due to the growth in years of education (see his *Sources of Economic Growth in the United States,* Committee for Economic Development, Washington, 1962). His Table 33 fixes the contribution of education at more than 40 per cent, but it is clear from his derivation that half of that was due to the increase in the number of days of attendance in each school year, which should *not* be excluded from our adjustment.

Total private costs of attending college can be considered the sum of private direct and indirect costs. The former includes tuition, fees, outlays on books and supplies, and any living expenses beyond what would be incurred when not in college. Average tuition and fees per college student in 1939 and other years can be estimated without too much trouble from data collected by the Office of Education. Books and unusual living expenses can be estimated from other surveys, notably a large national sample taken by the Education Office in 1950's. Private direct costs per student averaged about $173 in 1939, of which 65 per cent or $112 were tuition and fees.

Since students earn less than if they were participating full time in the labor force, the earnings foregone are an indirect cost of schooling. The amount foregone depends both on the number of hours spent at school work, and the opportunities for part-time (after school) and seasonal (summer) work. The latter determinant is quite sensitive to business conditions and the age, race, sex, etc., of students, so indirect costs vary more over time and among demographic groups than direct costs do.[5]

Indirect costs were estimated by assuming that the typical person attends college from the age of 18 to 22½ and earns one-quarter of what he could have earned. Four and a half years of college are assumed because the Census group with "16+" years of schooling ap-

---

[5] For the purpose of estimating rates of return, it is only necessary to recognize—as every one must—that students earn less than if they were participating in the labor force. This difference in earnings need not be called a cost of education nor related to direct costs. However, foregone earnings are treated as a cost here and throughout the book, because such a treatment adds to the understanding of the economic effects of education (and other human capital). Moreover, the arguments advanced against doing so cannot withstand close scrutiny. To take one prominent example, John Vaizey, who has written extensively on the economic effects of education, in arguing against the inclusion of foregone earnings, said: " . . . for young people there is no alternative; the law forbids them to work," or " . . . if income foregone is added to education costs it must also be added to other sectors of the economy (notably housewives, mothers, unpaid sitters-in, voluntary work of all sorts) . . . " and "Analytically, too, it would be necessary to adjust the costs by some notional estimate of benefits incurred while being educated . . . " (see his *The Economics of Education,* Glencoe, 1962, pp. 42-43). Now if foregone earnings are excluded because schooling is compulsory, surely direct costs have to be excluded also. If the foregone earnings of other activities are important, then, of course, they should be treated as costs too (and are in my paper *A Theory of the Allocation of Time,* IBM Research Paper RC-1149, March 20, 1964). Finally, that benefits are incurred while being educated is no more an argument against the inclusion of indirect costs than against the inclusion of direct costs.

pears to have that much undergraduate and postgraduate training.[6] The one-quarter assumption is based on the notion that college attendance is a full-time occupation for three-quarters of a year—vacations occupying the remaining quarter—for which notion there is direct evidence provided by several studies.[7] In principle, the potential earnings of first-year college students should be measured by the actual earnings of otherwise equivalent persons who entered the full-time labor force after completing high school, the potential earnings of second-year students by the actual earnings of otherwise equivalent persons who entered the labor force after completing one year of college, and so on. Limitations of data necessitated the use of a simpler, but not too inaccurate, method. The potential earnings of students during the first four years of college were measured by the actual earnings of "equivalent" high-school graduates of the same age, and potential earnings during the last half year of study by the earnings of college drop-outs of the same age.

The bottom half of Table 1 shows absolute and percentage differentials from ages 18 to 22 between the net earnings of college students and high-school graduates. "Net" earnings means that direct college costs have been subtracted from the earnings of college students. The total private cost of attending college for the average urban native-white male in 1939 is roughly measured by the series of absolute differentials. Foregone earnings account for about 74 per cent of the total, tuition and fees only about 17 per cent, and other direct costs the remaining 9 per cent. Therefore, if tuition and fees alone were eliminated—if colleges were made "free" in the usual meaning of this term—only a relatively small part of the private burden of attending college would be eliminated. That is to say, even at the private level "free" colleges are not really very free after all!

RATES OF RETURN IN 1939

The monetary gain from attending college can be determined from a comparison of returns and costs. A person deciding whether or not college "pays" should discount both the streams of returns and costs in order to incorporate the basic economic fact that $1,000 promised in ten years is worth less than $1,000 available today. Discounting of future income is incorporated into the internal rate of return, which

[6] See P. C. Glick and H. P. Miller, "Education Level and Potential Income," *American Sociological Review*, June 1956, p. 311.

[7] See Appendix A, section 2a.

is simply a rate of discount that makes the series of absolute earnings differentials between college and high-school graduates sum to zero.[8] One could also compute the present value of the monetary gain, which is the sum of all absolute differentials *after* they have been discounted at appropriate market interest rates (see Chapter III). Both methods are used in this chapter, although greatest attention is paid to the internal rate.

Since the concern is with the gain achieved by cohorts, the data in Table 1 have to be adjusted for mortality, growth, and taxation. Note that both measures of monetary gain use absolute, not percentage, earning differentials, so any adjustment changing the former would change the estimated gain, even if the latter were not changed. Thus the adjustments for mortality and growth do not change percentage differentials, but, as shall be seen, they do significantly alter the estimated gain. Note further that the rate of return to a cohort can be computed either from the stream of total (cohort) absolute differentials or from the mean (i.e., per capita) differentials. Likewise, the present value of the gain can be computed either from total differentials or on a per member basis from mean differentials. There has been considerable controversy over whether mean or median differentials are the more appropriate measure of the central tendency of returns (and presumably also of costs) to education. Means are clearly more appropriate when calculating *cohort* gains; perhaps medians are better for other purposes.[9]

Table 2 presents several alternative estimates of the private rate of

TABLE 2

ALTERNATIVE ESTIMATES OF RATES OF RETURN TO 1939 COHORT
OF NATIVE-WHITE MALE COLLEGE GRADUATES
(per cent)

Secular Rate of Growth in Earnings (per cent)	Straight 4 Per Cent Tax Rate (1)	1949 Actual Tax Rates (2)
2	16.8	15.3
1	15.6	14.1
0	14.4	13.0

[8] The internal rate does not, however, necessarily equate the present values of returns and costs (see the discussion in Chapter III).

[9] Edward Renshaw prefers the median to the mean for reasons I find largely unconvincing. See his "Estimating the Returns to Education," *Review of Economics and Statistics,* August 1960, p. 322.

return to the cohort of urban native-white males graduating from college in 1939. The estimates increase a little over 1 percentage point for each percentage point of increase in the secular growth in earnings, and are about 1.5 percentage points lower when the tax rates prevailing in 1949 are used in place of those in 1939. A figure of slightly over 14.5 per cent is probably the best single estimate of the rate. This figure and indeed *all* the estimates indicate a very substantial private gain to white male college graduates.

The dominance of foregone earnings and the relative unimportance of tuition can be vividly demonstrated with rate of return calculations. The gain from attending college would, of course, increase if any component of cost decreased. But while the complete elimination of tuition would increase the rate of return to these college graduates only by a little over 1 percentage point, the elimination of foregone earnings would almost double it. Thus, good economic reasons, as well as lack of information and motivation, may prevent poorer high-school graduates from attending even tuition-free colleges. The elimination of foregone earnings, which incidentally has never been tried on a large scale in the United States, should have a much greater effect on their incentive to go to college.

TABLE 3

EARNING DIFFERENTIALS BETWEEN
WHITE MALE COLLEGE AND HIGH-SCHOOL
GRADUATES IN 1949 AT VARIOUS AGES

Age	Percentage (1)	Absolute (2)
23–24	−16	−372
25–29	+8	+230
30–34	42	1,440
35–44	86	3,419
45–54	100	4,759
55–64	85	4,068
18–19	−111	−1,073
20–21	−95	−1,647
22	−59	−1,324

Source: United States Census of Population: 1950,
Special Reports—Education, Bureau of the Census,
Washington, 1953, Vol. IV, part 5, chapter B, Table 12.
Cost estimates used in the bottom half of the table were
obtained by the methods discussed in Appendix A.

77

Independent estimates of the rate of return to college graduates can be based on data collected by the 1950 Census. Table 3 presents absolute and percentage differentials between the net incomes of college and high-school graduates in 1949, where net income means that direct costs have been subtracted from the earnings of college graduates at ages 18 to 22½. I tried to approximate the returns and costs of the cohort of persons graduating from college about 1949 by adjusting these figures for mortality, growth, and taxation. The mortality adjustment was based on rates prevailing in 1949, and income differentials were again assumed to grow at a little over 1 per cent per annum. The tax adjustment was based on the incidence of the personal income tax in 1949, although a somewhat greater adjustment would be more appropriate as taxes have risen a little since 1949. No adjustment for unemployment is necessary since 1949 was a rather normal economic year.

The private rate of return to the 1949 cohort would be 12.7 per cent if income differentials grew at 1 per cent per annum, and about 1 percentage point higher or lower if they grew at 2 per cent or not at all. Probably the best single estimate is close to 13 per cent, somewhat lower than the 14.5 per cent estimate based on the 1940 Census data. Their general agreement increases the confidence that can be placed in the statistical (as opposed to conceptual) reliability of our calculations.

Is the slight decline between 1939 and 1949 indicative of a general secular decline in the monetary gain from education? Secular changes are discussed in Chapter VI, so now I shall only consider whether the apparent decline is spurious owing to a shift in the statistical base. The 1949 data refer to the total incomes of all whites while the 1939 data refer only to the earnings of urban native whites. For obvious reasons, the inclusion of property income raises the estimated return in 1949, although probably not by very much (see Appendix A). While the direction and, a fortiori, the magnitude of the effect of the other differences is more difficult to determine,[10] they probably cannot fully explain the apparent decline during the 1940's.

---

[10] For example, rural and foreign-born whites generally have less education, lower incomes at each education level, and a lower return from additional education than urban native whites do. The first two factors would increase, the third decrease, the rate of return estimated for 1949.

Rates of Return from College Education

2. Some Conceptual Difficulties

CORRELATION BETWEEN "ABILITY" AND EDUCATION

Although the similarity between the estimates derived from the 1940 and 1950 Censuses should increase one's confidence in the statistical foundations of the analysis, it does not make the conceptual foundations any firmer. And the technique of estimating the private rate of return on education from income differentials between persons differing in education has been repeatedly and strongly attacked. Simply worded, the argument is that the true rate of return on education is grossly overestimated because persons differing in education also differ in many characteristics that cause their incomes to differ systematically. By explicitly considering the variation in earnings with age and by restricting the analysis to persons of a given sex, race, and in 1939 urban-rural and nativity status, I have already managed to eliminate the more important demographic sources of bias.

Unquestionably the most serious remaining difficulty results from the presumed positive correlation between education and "ability," which has been argued with fervor by intelligent persons in the United States and many other countries. Moreover, the theory developed earlier implies that abler persons invest more in themselves, at least when "ability" is defined in an economic sense (see Chapter III, section 3). Finally, the available quantitative materials definitely show a positive relation between education and several measures of ability. Table 4 summarizes some evidence on the abilities of high-school and college persons in the United States in recent years. In columns 1 and 2 "intelligence" is measured by the average I.Q. (intelligence quotient) and the fraction with high I.Q.'s; in column 3 a combination of intelligence, interest in schooling, and perseverance is measured by the average rank in high school; and in column 4 a combination of "contacts," tastes, and knowledge about better-paying occupations is measured by the fraction with fathers in professional, semiprofessional, and managerial occupations. All suggest significantly greater ability among college than high-school graduates: an average I.Q. about 13 per cent higher, over twice the rate of I.Q.'s above 120, a 50 per cent higher class ranking in high school, and a 100 per cent larger number with fathers in the top occupations.

Although general observation, theoretical analysis, and quantitative evidence suggest a strong correlation between ability and education, what can be said about the magnitude of the bias in rate of return

TABLE 4

SEVERAL MEASURES OF ABILITY AT DIFFERENT EDUCATIONAL LEVELS IN THE 1950'S

Education	Average I.Q.[a] (1)	Percentage with I.Q. Over 120[a] (2)	Average Rank in High-School Graduating Class[b] (percentile) (3)	Percentage with Fathers in Professional, Semiprofessional, or Managerial Occupations[c] (4)
High-school graduate	106.8	20.8	44	22
College graduate	120.5	50.0	68	45
College drop-out	106.2	16.3	48	44

Source: Dael Wolfle, <u>America's Resources of Specialized Talent</u>, New York, 1954. Cols. 1-3 computed from Table G.2, p. 314, and Table H.1, p. 316; col. 4 computed from Table VI.6, p. 160, and Table VI.7, p. 162.

[a]The I.Q. estimates, based on the Army General Classification Test, are for 1953 and were based partly on special studies conducted by the Commission on Human Resources and partly on estimates made by others. Among the latter is the study by V. Benson, "The Intelligence and Later Scholastic Success of Sixth Grade Pupils," <u>School and Society</u>, February 1942. Her data are especially interesting because the subsequent education of children receiving I.Q. tests in the sixth grade was determined. Therefore, the positive relation between I.Q. and education in her study--which shows differences similar to those given above--cannot be considered a consequence of the education itself.

[b]These data on grades are national estimates prepared by the Commission for 1953. Almost identical results are given in the Bureau of the Census study, <u>Factors Related to College Attendance of Farm and Nonfarm High School Graduates: 1960</u>, Series Census-ERS (P-27) No. 32, Washington, 1962, Table 8.

[c]The distributions by father's occupation omit children with fathers in farm occupations and are rough estimates prepared by the Commission from the 1950 Census. Similar differences by father's education and income are given in <u>School Enrollment and Education of Young Adults and Their Fathers: October 1960</u>, Bureau of the Census, Washington, 1961, Tables 9-10.

estimates based on the income differential approach used in the last section? In particular, is most of the apparently large return to college graduates due to their greater ability, or only, say, 10 per cent? Neither general observation nor theoretical analysis has much to suggest about this, so considerable reliance has to be placed on the limited quantitative evidence, derived from five main independent methods presented below. The evidence suggests that this correlation explains only a small part of the apparently large return. Let me point out, however, that the discussion in Chapter VI concludes (see section 1) that much of the large apparent return to primary and secondary school education does result from differential ability.

1. It would be desirable to recalculate the rates of return presented earlier after the data had been fully standardized for ability. Either the incomes of college graduates could be standardized for the distri-

bution of ability among high-school graduates, or the incomes of the latter could be standardized for the ability of the former. The first method would determine the rate of return to a typical high-school graduate who decided to enter college, while the second would indicate the rate actually received by a typical college graduate. The latter would be greater if college graduates were abler and if abler persons benefit more from college.

Table 4 indicates that rank in class is strongly related to extent of education, so its effects are considered first. A good source of information on the relation between rank and earnings is the study of college graduates employed by the Bell Telephone Co. Rank in college did not affect starting salaries much, but after fifteen years the employees who had been in the top two-fifths of their college class earned about 20 per cent more than those in the bottom two-fifths, and in later years the differences were still greater.[11] The differences after fifteen years seem to be a good measure of the average relation between college rank and earnings.[12]

According to column 3 of Table 4, the typical person who did not go to college after finishing high school ranked much lower in high school than persons who completed college. Presumably, the former would also have ranked much lower in college if he had gone on. Consequently, according to the Bell data, he would also have earned less, perhaps a good deal less, than college graduates actually do. To be concrete, he would have earned about 7 per cent less if the Bell data accurately measure the relation between college rank and earnings, and if high-school and college graduates would have had the same relative ranking in college as they had in high school.[13]

---

[11] See Donald S. Bridgman, "Success in College and Business," *The Personnel Journal,* June 1930. A more recent and comprehensive study, as yet unpublished, appears to give very similar results.

[12] If earnings of abler graduates rise more rapidly with age partly because of greater investment on the job and in other human capital (see Chapter II, section 1) the extent of the relation between rank and earnings would be underestimated by the differentials at younger ages and overestimated by those at older ages. Differentials after fifteen years of employment tend to avoid the extremes of either bias.

[13] If E_i is the average earnings of college graduates who were at the ith rank level in college, and if d_{ih} and d_{ic} give the proportion of college and high-school graduates who would have been at this level, the ratio of their earnings after college would be

$$p = \frac{\Sigma E_i d_{ih}}{\Sigma E_i d_{ic}}.$$

If E_1 covers the top two-fifths, E_2 the third fifth, and E_3 the bottom two-fifths, then,

Income differentials between college and high-school graduates would, therefore, significantly overstate the gain to a typical high-school graduate from completing college, for at ages 35-44 (roughly fifteen years after completing college) 7 per cent of college graduates' incomes equals almost 20 per cent of the apparent gain from college.[14] The rate of return estimates would be reduced by a smaller percentage. The best estimate of the private rate would be reduced from about 14.5 to a little over 12.5 per cent for the 1939 cohort and from 13 to about 11.5 per cent for the 1949 cohort, or an average reduction of about 12 per cent.[15]

2. An adjusted rate of return to a typical college graduate could be computed if the relation between rank and the earnings of high-school graduates were known. Unfortunately, the Bell study did not collect information on the earnings of high-school graduates. But this as well as other useful information can be found in a recent study of Wolfle and Smith.[16] They obtained annual salaries some fifteen to twenty years later of about 2,800 male graduates of high schools in Illinois, Minnesota, and Rochester, N. Y., in the middle and late 1930's. Most of the persons included from Illinois and Minnesota were in the upper 60 per cent, either in class standing or I.Q., while the Rochester sample (which was smaller) was limited to persons in the top 20 per cent on either measure.

The top panel of Table 5 presents the relation between percentile rank in high school, median earnings, and education for the whole

---

according to the Bell Telephone study, $E_1 = 1.18 \, E_3$ and $E_2 = 1.02 \, E_3$. Data from the Commission on Human Resources indicates that 68 per cent of persons graduating from college were in the top two-fifths of their high-school class, 17 per cent in the third fifth, and 14 per cent in the bottom two-fifths, while only 32 per cent of high-school graduates not going on to college were in the top two-fifths, 20 per cent were in the third fifth, and 48 per cent in the bottom two-fifths (see Wolfle, *America's Resources*, Appendix H, Table 1). Substituting these figures into the equation gives $p = .93$.

14 It is about 19 per cent of the apparent gain to the 1939 cohort of college graduates and 16 per cent of that to the 1949 cohort.

15 The adjusted rates probably should be slightly lower because the direct college costs of a typical high-school graduate were assumed to equal the actual average direct costs of college graduates, even though the former's tuition would probably be somewhat higher since colleges engage in "price discrimination" against persons with lower high-school ranks. Since the assumption that college students earn one-quarter of the amount earned by high-school graduates of the same age already incorporates a correction for the differential ability of college students (see Appendix A, section 2a), no adjustment of indirect costs would be necessary.

16 See D. Wolfle and J. Smith, "The Occupational Value of Education for Superior High School Graduates," *Journal of Higher Education,* April 1956, pp. 201-213.

Rates of Return from College Education

TABLE 5

MEDIAN SALARIES OF ILLINOIS, MINNESOTA, AND ROCHESTER MEN,
BY RANK IN HIGH-SCHOOL GRADUATING CLASS
AND BY INTELLIGENCE TEST SCORE
(dollars)

Ability Measure	Education		
	High School (1)	Some College (2)	One College Degree or More (3)
Percentile rank in high-school class[a]			
91-100	4,880	5,600	7,100
81- 90	4,780	5,400	6,300
71- 80	4,720	5,300	6,500
61- 70	4,810	5,700	5,700
1- 60	4,655	5,300	5,700
Intelligence test, percentile in sample[b]			
Highest 20	4,000	5,300	6,300
Next 35	4,500	5,200	6,100
Bottom 45	4,300	4,100	5,200
Intelligence quotient[c]			
Over 120	5,500	6,100	7,600
Under 120	5,000	5,700	7,400

Source: Dael Wolfle and Joseph Smith, "The Occupation Value of Education for Superior High-School Graduates," Journal of Higher Education, April 1956, pp. 201-213, Tables II, IV, and V.

[a]Illinois, Minnesota, and Rochester men.

[b]Minnesota men.

[c]Rochester men.

sample. The Bell study gives the relation of college rank, this one (in column 3) the relation of high-school rank, to the earnings of college graduates. Those at the top earn significantly more than those at the bottom of their high-school class, where the bottom 1-60 percentile class actually is largely restricted to persons in the 40-60 percentile class. Indeed, the relation of rank and the earnings of college graduates given here is almost exactly the same as that given in the Bell study. Fifteen years after graduation, persons who had been in the top two-fifths of their class were earning 16 per cent more than those in the third fifth, according to the latter study, and averaged about $6600, compared to the $5700 earned by those in the third fifth, according to the former study. Thus, rank-adjusted rates of return to typical high-school graduates computed from these data would be essentially the same as those computed earlier from the Bell study.

83

The stub entries in Table 5 provide the data necessary to compute rank-adjusted returns to typical college graduates. However, since there was little systematic relationship[17] between rank and the earnings of high-school graduates, no adjustment is required. The typical college graduate apparently receives a higher rate of return from college than would a typical high-school graduate, because the former has a higher class rank, and the pay-off from college is greater for those with higher ranks. Indeed, this greater pay-off is presumably an important reason why persons with higher class ranks go to college much more frequently than others do.[18]

The bottom two panels of Table 5 give the effect of I.Q. on earnings. The Rochester data are derived from a small and highly restrictive sample. The Minnesota data are more interesting since they cover persons with I.Q.'s mostly above the top 60th percentile of all high-school students. This sample indicates that an increase in I.Q. has the same kind of effect on earnings as an increase in rank: a negligible effect among high-school graduates[19] and a 15-20 per cent effect among college graduates. So an adjustment for I.Q. alone would reduce the apparent gain from college by about the same amount as the adjustment for rank did. These effects cannot, however, be added together to get the effect of simultaneously adjusting for rank and I.Q. since they are very highly correlated.[20] Therefore, adding an I.Q. adjustment to the rank adjustment would lower the rate of return to a typical high-school graduate probably by less than 0.5 of a percentage point: from 12.5 to 12.0 per cent for the 1939 cohort and from 11.5+ to 11+ per cent for the 1949 cohort. The rate of return to an average college graduate would hardly be reduced at all, and would remain near 14.5 and 13 per cent for the 1939 and 1949 cohorts, respectively.

17 At least within the top 60th percentile, which is essentially all that is relevant to the typical college graduate.

18 Almost 50 per cent in the top two-fifths of their high-school class go to college, while only 22 per cent in the bottom two-fifths go (see Wolfle, *America's Resources,* Table VI-2, p. 150). For similar results, see *Factors Related to College Attendance,* Table 9. Some studies indicate, moreover, that rank increases the likelihood of attending college even when the parents' economic position is held constant. See *ibid.,* Tables 14-16; also see some references in C. C. Cole, *Encouraging Scientific Talent,* New York, 1956, pp. 57 ff.

19 One should point out, however, that high-school graduates with high I.Q.'s and high grades may not go to college precisely because they rank low in other kinds of ability. This may explain why they do not earn much more than other high-school graduates.

20 See Wolfle, *America's Resources,* Appendix H, Table 1.

The Wolfle-Smith study also contains useful information on the relation between father's occupation, education, and earnings. Once again the effect is much greater at the college level. College graduates with fathers in professional or managerial occupations earned about 16 per cent more than those with fathers in unskilled or service occupations, while high-school graduates with fathers in top occupations earned only about 4 per cent more. Therefore, an adjustment for father's occupation alone would hardly reduce the gain to a typical college graduate and would reduce the gain from college to a typical high-school graduate by about 7 per cent.[21] Again, the high correlation between rank, I.Q., and father's occupation implies that the effect of adjusting for father's occupation, in addition to adjusting for rank and I.Q., would be much less than if it were the sole adjustment.

This discussion of the data provided by the Committee on Human Resources can now be summarized. Even if rank in high school, I.Q., and father's occupation are adjusted for separately, the rate of return from college to a typical college graduate would hardly be affected, while that to a typical high-school graduate would be reduced by about 35 per cent. College education itself would be the major determinant of the apparently high return associated with education. Moreover, the sum of the separate effects grossly overstates the combined effect, since rank, I.Q., and father's occupation are quite closely correlated. Thus, the fraction of the unadjusted return attributable to college education itself would be very high.

3. J. Morgan and M. H. David recently published an interesting attempt to isolate the effect of education on earnings through standardization by multiple regression for other influences.[22] In one set of regressions, they adjusted the family earnings of white male heads of nonfarm households in the labor force for measures of religion, personality, father's education, labor market conditions, mobility, and supervisory responsibilities. The share of the unadjusted earnings

[21] The effect on income can be found from the formula in footnote 13 above where the index i would now refer to father's occupation rather than school rank. The distribution of high-school and college graduates by father's occupation can be found in Wolfle, *America's Resources,* Tables VI. 6 and VI. 7, pp. 160 and 162. Substituting these weights and the data on earnings given by Wolfle and Smith (*Journal of Higher Education,* April 1956) into the formula gives $p = .963$. The adjusted rate of return would then be estimated at a little more than 13.5 and 12 per cent instead of 14.5 and 13 per cent for the 1939 and 1949 cohorts.

[22] See their "Education and Income," *Quarterly Journal of Economics,* August 1963, pp. 423-437. The data were collected by the Survey Research Center from a national sample of approximately 3,000 heads of spending units.

differential between college and high-school graduates explained by these factors was about 40 per cent at ages 18-34 and 12 per cent at ages 35-74.[23] In other regressions, measures of rank in school and ability to understand and answer questions were of negligible importance.[24] Hence, in their sample too, college education itself is the major cause of differentials between college and high-school graduates, especially when one recognizes—as Morgan and David do—that supervisory responsibility and mobility are primarily simply means through which the economic effects of education operate.[25]

4. A very different way to eliminate the influence of several dimensions of ability is to consider the earnings of college drop-outs. Table 4 indicates that college entrants who drop out before completing four years do not have higher I.Q.'s or grades than high-school graduates. True, the same table indicates that the former came from higher social and economic backgrounds, but they were unable to finish an activity that they had started,[26] and so their advantage may be counterbalanced by lack of sustained effort. College drop-outs, therefore, do not seem to have much, if any, greater "ability" than high-school

23 See *ibid.*, Table III. These results refer to college graduates with a bachelor's degree only and high-school graduates without any nonacademic (presumably formal) training. The results for persons with advanced degrees and nonacademic training are about the same. However, differentials between all college and all high-school graduates could not be computed because the number of cases in each group was not given.

24 *Ibid*, pp. 428-429. For an earlier and in some ways more complete discussion, see J. Morgan, M. H. David, W. J. Cohen, and H. E. Brazer, *Income and Welfare in the United States*, New York, 1962, Chapter 5.

25 In general, when standardizing by multiple regression or some other technique to obtain the effect of education on earnings, one must be careful not to go too far. For education has little direct effect on earnings; it operates primarily indirectly through the effect on knowledge and skills. Consequently, by standardizing for enough measures of knowledge and skill, such as occupation or ability to communicate, one can eliminate the entire true effect of education on earnings.

This comment is relevant not only to the Morgan-David study, but also to several others, such as a recent interesting dissertation by Shane Hunt (see "Income Determinants for College Graduates and the Return to Educational Investment," unpublished Ph.D. dissertation, Yale University, 1963). He utilizes a survey in 1947 by *Time* magazine of the incomes of college graduates and finds that graduates of relatively expensive colleges received about a 12 per cent crude rate of return on their additional costs, i.e., those not incurred by graduates of relatively cheap colleges. After standardization for several variables, he cuts the rate substantially. Among those held constant, however, are variables, like occupational category, which clearly partly measure the way in which education affects earnings. Nevertheless, even after all his adjustments, higher-quality college education still yields a significant gain, which is about half the crude gain.

26 Of course, some persons discontinuing school after graduation from junior college, because of marriage, etc., may not have planned to finish four years of college.

graduates (see the discussion in section 3 below). If so, unadjusted rates of return to drop-outs would in effect already standardize for ability and would not overestimate the true pay-off to some college.

In section 3 below unadjusted rates of return to the 1939 and 1949 cohorts of college drop-outs are estimated at about 9.5 and 8 per cent, respectively. Even if these are used to measure the adjusted gain to college graduates, almost two-thirds[27] of the apparent gain from college can be attributed to the education itself. Moreover, the adjusted gain to graduates is probably still larger because the gain from the third, fourth, and later college years is somewhat greater than that from earlier years (see section 3 below).

5. A study during the late 1920's adjusted for ability in a rather unique way, namely, by considering the incomes of brothers with different amounts of education.[28] Since brothers come from the same economic and social background, and presumably differ less in native ability than typical elementary, high-school, and college persons, many kinds of ability often considered important in explaining earning differentials would be held constant. On the other hand, some brothers may become relatively well-educated precisely because of unusual ambition and other kinds of ability rather than because of interest, "luck," and other factors uncorrelated with earnings. Therefore, the study probably does not entirely correct for differences in ability.

Tables 16 and 17 in Chapter VI indicate that the effect of education on income was substantial among these brothers: for example, those averaging 15.5 years of schooling earned about $834 more than those averaging 10.8 years, or about $175 per school year. Lacking reliable income data for the 1920's, this gain will be compared with the unadjusted gain in 1939. One difficulty here is that the Census data are known to understate earnings and to omit the foreign-born, the self-employed, and some other categories of whites, while the biases in the data on the brothers are not known. So the brothers' differentials will be compared with both raw and corrected Census differentials. In 1939 prices the brothers' gain at ages 30-34 would be 67 per cent of the gain per school year to college graduates based on 1940 Census data corrected for underreporting of earnings and independent professionals, and 81 per cent of the uncorrected gain. So

---

[27] That is, $9.5 \div 14.5 = .65$ and $8 \div 13 = .62$.

[28] See Donald E. Gorseline, *The Effect of Schooling Upon Income*, Bloomington, 1932.

these data also indicate that college education itself explains most of the apparent gain to college graduates.[29]

Five independent adjustments for differential ability—adjustments that cover such diverse influences as rank in class, I.Q., father's education and occupation, personality, ability to communicate, motivation, and family upbringing—all suggest that college education itself explains most of the unadjusted earnings differential between college and high-school graduates. Although any one study is subject to many qualifications, the evidence provided by all taken together has to be given considerable weight. Consequently, it may be concluded that, even after adjustment for differential ability, the private rate of return to a typical white male college graduate would be considerable, say, certainly more than 10 per cent.

A reader might well wonder how this conclusion squares with the evidence, from general observations and theory, advanced earlier that ability and education are quite highly correlated. These observations may have been based primarily on relations below the college level,[30] and as already pointed out, the discussion later on (in Chapter VI) indicates that differential ability has a greater impact there. The theory developed in Part One suggests a positive correlation between ability and education, in that high-school graduates who go to college would receive a higher rate of return from college than graduates who do not go. The limited evidence available supports this suggestion, for data from the Commission on Human Resources do indicate that a typical college graduate gains more from college than would a typical person dropping out after completing high school. Even the latter, however, would receive a high rate of return.

CORRELATION BETWEEN EDUCATION AND OTHER HUMAN CAPITAL

A correlation between the amount invested in education and in on-the-job and vocational training, health, and other human capital would also affect the earning differentials between education classes.

---

[29] Since these brothers were on the average only about 30 years old, perhaps their gain should be compared to that received by the Census category aged 25-29. Such a comparison would increase the fraction of the Census differentials attributable to college education itself. On the other hand, brothers with more education were about two years older on the average than those with less education, so the apparent effect of more education is in part an effect of older age.

[30] A more cynical explanation would be that vocal observers are themselves primarily successful college graduates and, therefore, naturally biased toward the view that ability is a major cause of the high earnings received by college graduates.

The effect of education itself could be isolated only if the amount of other human capital as well as ability were held constant. This section considers the effect on the apparent gain from education of adjusting for the relation between education and other capital.

The empirical evidence available here is even more limited than that available on differential ability. More than half of all high-school graduates in the sample from three states compiled by the Commission on Human Resources had some technical school training.[31] Although the Commission presented no evidence on this, such training is probably less common among college graduates. Other studies indicate that on-the-job training and expenditures on health, adult education, and migration are greater among college than among high-school graduates.[32] College graduates seem, therefore, also to invest more in other human capital than high-school graduates, although the opposite is clearly true for some kinds of capital, and a fuller treatment would have to incorporate these differences.

However, the net effect of even a positive correlation between education and other human capital on the earning differentials between college and high-school graduates may contradict the reader's intuitive presumption. Consider college graduates who received on-the-job training from, say, the age of 24 to 30; after that age they would earn more than if they had had no training, but they would earn less during the training period because training costs are then paid by a reduction in reported earnings (see Chapter II, section 1). Training, and, more generally all other investments in human capital, would therefore increase observed differentials at older ages and reduce them at younger ones, the net effect depending on the relation between deducted costs and returns from the investments, and the rate at which future earnings are discounted. Deducted costs may be less than actual costs because the direct costs of health, migration, and certain other investments are not deducted from earnings. This consideration

31 See Wolfle and Smith, *Journal of Higher Education,* April 1956.

32 Indirect estimates of the relation between on-the-job training and education were prepared by J. Mincer in "On-the-Job Training: Costs, Returns, and Some Implications," *Investment in Human Beings,* NBER Special Conference 15, Supplement to *Journal of Political Economy,* October 1962, Tables 1 and 2. Evidence on the relation between health and education is cited by S. Mushkin (*ibid.,* p. 131). Evidence indicating a strong positive correlation between adult education and formal education can be found in J. W. C. Johnstone, *Volunteers for Learning,* National Opinion Research Center, Report No. 89, Chicago, 1963. Tabulations from the 1950 Census indicate that more educated persons have higher migration rates (computed by June Cohn for the Labor Workshop at Columbia University).

is not too important, since foregone earnings are usually the main component of costs.

If the rate of return on other investments was the same as the rate on education, the rate computed from the education-earnings differentials would equal the true rate on education, and thus would *not* be biased. This rate would make the present value of the gross differentials equal to zero because it makes both the present value of the differentials due to other investments and those due to education equal to zero. If the rates of return on other investments were smaller than the rate on education, the rate computed from the gross differentials would also be smaller than the true rate on education, still assuming that education and other investments were positively correlated. For the rate on education would make the present value of the differentials due to other investments negative. Conversely, if the rates of return on other investments were larger, the rate computed from the gross differentials would also be larger than the true rate on education. The opposite conclusions hold if education and other investments are negatively correlated.

Thus, rates of return computed from gross differentials could be seriously biased estimates of the true rates on education only if the rates of return on education and other human capital differed considerably. Moreover, even if education and other capital were very positively correlated, computed rates could *understate* the true rates on education, and would do so whenever the latter were greater than the rates on other capital.

A priori arguments are ambiguous and do not indicate whether rates on education are higher or lower than those on other human capital.[33] Unfortunately, moreover, few empirical studies of rates of return on other human capital have been made; some preliminary estimates by Mincer suggest higher rates on college education than on other capital.[34] If so, rates computed from differentials between college and high-school graduates would be biased *downward* if the former also invested more in other kinds of human capital.

3. Rates of Return to Other College Persons

White male college graduates make up less than a third of all persons who receive some college education; about half of those starting col-

---

[33] See Mincer in *Investment in Human Beings*, pp. 63-64.
[34] *Ibid.*, pp. 64-65.

lege drop out before completing four years, and more than a third of all graduates are female or nonwhite.[35] Therefore, the average gain from college would be seriously overstated by estimates based on white male graduates if, as is often alleged, they gain much more from college than drop-outs, nonwhites, or females.[36] This section discusses the gains to drop-outs, nonwhites, women, and rural persons, and concludes that they are smaller than the gain to urban white male graduates, although the differences are less than is often alleged. Also considered are discrimination against nonwhites, the relationship between marriage and education, some historical testimony on the importance of foregone earnings, and an indirect method of assessing relative gains.

COLLEGE DROP-OUTS

If college graduates were more successful than the average person with some college, concentration on graduates alone would overestimate the gain to all persons with some college, in the same way that concentration on long-running plays alone would overestimate the gain from investing in Broadway plays. As already mentioned, a bias here could be important since almost half of all males starting college drop out before completing four years, and some writers have implied that the gain to drop-outs is substantially less than that to graduates. To take an extreme case, if the rate of return to drop-outs were zero,[37] the rate to all persons entering college would be about two-thirds that

---

[35] See Robert E. Ibbert, *Retention and Withdrawal of College Students,* U.S. Office of Education, Washington, 1957, Table 8, p. 18, and *Population Characteristics, Educational Attainment: March 1957,* Current Population Reports of the Bureau of the Census, Series P-20, No. 77, Tables B-C, 2, 3, and 4.

[36] "Furthermore, the statistics show that graduation at any level yields a bonus amounting to about twice the investment realized by the average man who starts a given type of school (elementary school, high school or college) but does not finish." (Glick and Miller, *American Sociological Review,* June 1956, p. 309). Or, as H. Houthakker said, "Hence it may not be true, in the case of higher learning, that it is better to have loved and lost than never to have loved at all" ("Education and Income," *Review of Economics and Statistics,* February 1959, p. 27). For views on the relative gains to Negroes and women, see Morgan and David, *Quarterly Journal of Economics,* August 1963, p. 437, and H. Schaffer, "Investment in Human Capital: Comment," *American Economic Review,* December 1961, pp. 1031-1032.

[37] This is not the most extreme case, since the rate could be negative, and would be if the sum of returns were less than the sum of costs.

91

of graduates,[38] or less than 10 per cent for the 1939 and 1949 cohorts. Consequently, if college were of no economic value to drop-outs, the rate of return on college would begin to seem rather modest.

Drop-outs earn relatively little more than high-school graduates, which explains why their gain is quite often considered small. In 1949, for example, the average income of white male high-school graduates aged 35-44 was about 60 per cent of that of college graduates and 80 per cent of that of college drop-outs the same age. However, one must not forget that costs are also less for drop-outs since they average only about two years of college,[39] while graduates average about four and a half years. The rate of return would be lower for drop-outs only if the difference in returns were greater than the difference in costs. Depending on the adjustment for growth and taxation, the private

[38] The rate of return can be approximated by $r = k/C$, where r is the rate for the cohort, k the average return per period, and C is the sum of costs (see Chapter III, section 1). Let the subscripts g, d, and a refer to graduates, drop-outs, and all entrants, respectively; since by assumption $r_d = 0$, then $k_d = 0$. If drop-outs attend college for two years on the average and are equal in number to graduates, then

$$k_a = 0 + k_g, \text{ and } C_a = C_g + \frac{4}{9} C_g = \frac{13}{9} C_g.$$

Therefore, $$r_a = k_a/C_a = k_g / \frac{13}{9} C_g = \frac{9}{13} k_g/C_g = \frac{9}{13} r_g.$$

[39] The Office of Education followed a sample of students entering college in 1950 for four years (see *Retention and Withdrawal of College Students*). Persons dropping out of their institution of first registration averaged about 1.4 years of school (estimated from *ibid.*, Table 8). This underestimates the average college education of the Census category 13-15 years of schooling for two major reasons. The Office of Education study refers only to drop-outs from the institution of first registration, yet 17 per cent of these were known to have transferred to other institutions before the fall of 1954 (*ibid.*, p. 81). In addition, the Census category is supposed to include only persons who have completed at least thirteen years and less than sixteen years of schooling. If persons dropping out before *completing* the first year were omitted from the special study, drop-outs would average about 2.4 years of college. Some other biases, however, work in the opposite direction. For example, transferees eventually completing college presumably average more years of college initially than other drop-outs. More importantly, the special study only includes colleges offering a four-year program. Graduates and drop-outs from junior colleges have no more than two years of schooling from their institution of first registration. I decided to split the difference between 1.4 and 2.4 and take 2 years as the average college education of persons reporting 13-15 years of schooling.

Some supporting evidence is given in a tabulation of the number of persons completing 13, 14, or 15 years of schooling. If all persons in this category dropped out just after completing a year, the 13-15 category would average about 13.8 years; if they dropped out in midyear, they would average 14.3 years (computed from *Population Characteristics, Educational Attainment: March 1957*, Table D).

rate of return would range from 8.2 to 11.6 per cent for the 1939 cohort of urban, native-white, male college drop-outs and from 6.6 to 8.7 per cent for the 1949 cohort of white male drop-outs, with the best single estimates at about 9.5 and 8 per cent, respectively (see the discussion in section 1 above). These rates are far from negligible and indicate that some college is by no means an economic waste. At the same time they are decidedly less than the corresponding rates of 14.5 and 13 per cent for college graduates, and suggest that the difference in costs does not completely offset the difference in returns. According to these estimates the last two and a half years of college would yield about 18 per cent,[40] while the rate for all entrants would be some 1.5 percentage points less than that for graduates.[41]

As already mentioned, these unadjusted rates of return to college drop-outs may not be biased upward since drop-outs have about the same I.Q. and class rank as high-school graduates (see Table 4), and while drop-outs come from higher socioeconomic backgrounds, they have demonstrated a certain lack of persistence. This view receives support from the study by Morgan and David referred to in section 2 above: differentials between college drop-outs and high-school graduates after adjustment for a measure of socioeconomic background and other variables are almost as large as or perhaps even larger than the unadjusted differentials.[42] On the other hand, the discussion in section 2 indicates that the crude rates of return to college graduates are somewhat biased upward. One set of adjustments for class rank and I.Q. reduced the gain from college to a typical high-school graduate from about 13.5 per cent to slightly under 11.5 per cent, which eliminates almost half of the crude difference in rates between graduates and drop-outs. Adjustments performed by Morgan and David also reduce but do not eliminate the differential between graduates and

[40] The rate on all four and a half years is approximately a simple average of those for each year (see Chapter III, section 1, especially fn. 7).

[41] Using the notation and assumptions of fn. 38 gives $C_a = C_g + C_d$, $k_a = k_g + k_d$, and, therefore,

$$r_a = \frac{k_a}{C_a} = \frac{k_g + k_d}{C_g + C_d} = r_g \frac{C_g}{C_g + C_d} + r_d \frac{C_d}{C_g + C_d} = w r_g + (1 - w) r_d.$$

If $r_g = 13\frac{1}{2}$ per cent and $r_d = 8\frac{1}{2}$ per cent, r_a is approximately 12 per cent since w is about 9/13.

[42] The ratio of unadjusted to adjusted differentials is 87 per cent at ages 18-34 and 113 per cent at older ages (see *Quarterly Journal of Economics*, August 1963, Table III). Moreover, in some ways the unadjusted differentials were overadjusted (see my comments on their study in section 2).

drop-outs.[43] Consequently, much, although not all, of the very large apparent bonus for college graduation would seem to result from the differential ability of college graduates. The remaining bonus may indicate some "increasing returns" to the third, fourth, and later years of college study.

NONWHITES

Absolute income differentials between college and high-school graduates are substantially less for nonwhites than for whites: for example, in 1939 nonwhite male college graduates aged 35-44 earned about $700 more in the South and $500 more in the North than nonwhite high-school graduates, about one-third of the $2,000 differential for whites. Nonwhites do not necessarily gain less from college, however, since both their direct and indirect college costs are much lower. Indirect costs are lower because nonwhite high-school graduates earn less than white graduates, and direct costs are lower because nonwhites attend cheaper (and "lower-quality") colleges.[44] Again the relevant question is whether the difference in costs is sufficient to compensate for the difference in returns. Depending on the adjustments for taxes and growth, the 1939 cohort of urban, nonwhite, male college graduates received rates of return ranging from 10.6 to 14 per cent in the South, and from 6.6 to 10 per cent in the North, with the best estimates at about 12.3 and 8.3 per cent.[45] Both are less than the 14.5 per cent rate for urban native-white males.[46] This evidence indicates that non-

---

[43] *Ibid.* They were reduced by 65 and 14 per cent at ages 18-34 and 35-74, respectively.

[44] Most nonwhites are Negroes and about 85 per cent of Negro college students in 1947 were enrolled in Negro colleges (see *Higher Education for American Democracy*, A Report of the President's Commission on Higher Education, Washington, 1947, Vol. II, p. 31). In 1940 the average expenditure per student in Negro colleges was only about 70 per cent of that in white colleges. For white costs, see *Current Operating Expenditures and Income of Higher Education in the United States, 1930, 1940 and 1950,* Commission on Financing Higher Education, New York, 1952, Tables 58 and 3; for Negro costs, see "Statistics of Higher Education, 1939-40," *Biennial Survey of Education in the U.S., 1938-40,* Washington, 1944, Vol. II, Chapter IV, Tables 18 and 19. For some complaints about the low quality of Negro colleges, see the article by F. M. Hechinger in *The New York Times,* Sept. 22, 1963.

[45] All nonwhite graduates are assumed to go to Negro colleges, which was nearly true of nonwhites in the South and largely true of those in the North. If northern nonwhites went to white colleges, their rate of return would only be about 7.3 per cent.

[46] None of these rates have been adjusted for differential ability because the relevant data are not available for nonwhites. Their *differential* ability is probably greater than that for whites because only the more ambitious and otherwise able nonwhites can overcome their very low socioeconomic background and go on to college. If so, adjusted rates would be relatively lower for nonwhites.

white male high-school graduates have less incentive than white graduates, but not much less, to go to college.

One way to check such a conclusion, as well as to provide indirect evidence on rates of return when direct evidence is not available, is to look at actual behavior. Each group of high-school graduates can be said to have a curve relating the fraction going to college to the gain expected from college. Presumably these curves are positively inclined, and their location and elasticity are determined, respectively, by the average level and the dispersion around the average in ability, availability of financing, tastes, and attitudes toward risk. If two groups had identical supply curves, the gain expected by one would be larger if, and only if, the fraction going to college were also larger.

Now if white and nonwhite males had identical supply curves, the modestly higher rate of return estimated for whites would imply—if the elasticity was of medium size—that a modestly larger fraction of whites would go to college.[47] Many readers may be surprised to learn that almost as many nonwhite high-school graduates go to college as white: in 1957, about one-third of all nonwhite male high-school graduates over 25 had some college, while a little over two-fifths of all white male graduates did.[48] Of course, the fact that fewer nonwhites go to college cannot be considered impressive support of the evidence indicating that nonwhites gain less. For their supply curve has probably been to the left of that of whites,[49] and thus fewer nonwhites would go to college even if the gains were the same. But the relatively small difference in the fractions going to college is impressive support of the evidence indicating that the difference in gains is not very great. For *many fewer* nonwhites would go to college if their supply curve were much to the left *and* if they gained much less from college.[50]

[47] Of course, the quantity supplied would be a function of the expected real gain, not merely the monetary gain. In relating relative supplies to relative monetary gains, I am implicitly assuming that any differences in psychic gains can be ignored. See Chapter V for a further discussion of psychic gains and their relation to actual behavior.

[48] See *Population Characteristics, Educational Attainment: March 1957*, Tables 1 and 3.

[49] Nonwhites typically have less resources, and experience greater difficulty in gaining admission to certain colleges.

[50] Moreover, there is some evidence that fewer nonwhite male graduates generally go to college even when father's education and several other variables are held constant (see *School Enrollment, and Education of Young Adults and Their Fathers: October 1960*, Current Population Reports, Washington, 1961, Table 9; and *Factors*

Discrimination Against Nonwhites[51]

It may be surprising that the rate of return to nonwhite college graduates appears lower in the North than in the South and only slightly lower than the rate of return to whites, since discrimination is clearly much greater in the South and increases in both regions with the education of nonwhites.[52] In this section, rate of return estimates are related to the analysis of discrimination, thus reconciling the findings here with my earlier work on discrimination. The main result of this reconciliation is to support the implications of the rate of return estimates; namely, discrimination against nonwhite college graduates may have been less in the South than in the North and relatively modest, especially in the South.

The market discrimination coefficient (MDC) between two groups has been defined as[53]

$$MDC = \frac{\pi_w}{\pi_n} - \frac{\pi_w^0}{\pi_n^0}, \tag{34}$$

where π_w and π_n are actual earnings and π_w^0 and π_n^0 are what they would be in the absence of market discrimination. If these groups were equally productive, $\pi_n^0 = \pi_w^0$, and

$$MDC = \frac{\pi_w}{\pi_n} - 1. \tag{35}$$

If several sets of these groups can be distinguished by an ordered characteristic, such as occupation, education, age, or income, the MDC can be said to measure average discrimination, and a marginal MDC measuring the additional discrimination encountered as a result of moving to a higher level can be defined in terms of the change in earnings between levels, as:

Related to College Attendance of Farm and Nonfarm High School Graduates: 1960, U.S. Bureau of the Census, Washington, 1962, Table 16). In general, nonwhites have been found to have less education even when many other factors are held constant (see M. H. David, H. Brazer, J. Morgan, and W. Cohen, *Educational Achievement— Its Causes and Effects*, Ann Arbor, 1961, Tables 1-10).

[51] This section deviates from the main line of argument and can be skipped by persons not especially concerned with discrimination against nonwhites.

[52] See my *Economics of Discrimination*, Chicago, 1957, Chapters 7-8.

[53] See *ibid.*, Chapter 2.

$$MDC_{ij} = \frac{\overset{j}{\pi_w} - \overset{i}{\pi_w}}{\overset{j}{\pi_n} - \overset{i}{\pi_n}} - \frac{\overset{0j}{\pi_w} - \overset{0i}{\pi_w}}{\overset{0j}{\pi_n} - \overset{0i}{\pi_n}}, \qquad (36)$$

where j and i are different levels of the characteristic in question. Equal productivity between W and N would give the simpler relation

$$MDC_{ij} = \frac{\overset{j}{\pi_w} - \overset{i}{\pi_w}}{\overset{j}{\pi_n} - \overset{i}{\pi_n}} - 1. \qquad (37)$$

Well-known relations between marginal and average functions imply that the marginal MDC would be above, equal to, or less than the average MDC depending on whether the latter was increasing, constant, or decreasing.

TABLE 6

AVERAGE AND MARGINAL MARKET DISCRIMINATION AGAINST NONWHITES FOR
VARIOUS AGE AND EDUCATION CLASSES, BY REGION, 1939

Age	Average MDC by Years of Education			Marginal MDC by Years of Education		Adjusted Marginal MDC by Years of Education	
	16+ (1)	12 (2)	7 & 8 (3)	16+ (4)	12 (5)	16+ (6)	12 (7)
			SOUTH				
25–29	.82	1.08	.69	.35	4.35	.37	3.57
30–34	1.27	1.23	.89	1.33	2.97	.43	2.65
35–44	1.50	1.68	1.12	1.23	4.49	.61	3.66
45–54	1.57	1.62	1.27	1.49	2.85	.69	2.57
55–64	1.56	1.55	1.08	1.62	3.61	.72	3.07
			NORTH				
25–29	.47	.50	.37	.37	1.23	.71	1.52
30–34	.78	.72	.45	.89	2.82	.99	2.61
35–44	1.17	.96	.64	1.75	2.70	1.44	2.53
45–54	1.37	.85	.73	3.92	1.17	2.58	1.48
55–64	1.23	.70	.63	5.11	.86	3.20	1.27

Source: Basic data from 16th Census of the United States: 1940, Population, Educational Attainment by Economic Characteristics and Marital Status, Bureau of the Census, Washington, 1947, Tables 29, 31, 33, 35. Zeman (in his unpublished Ph.D. dissertation, "A Quantitative Analysis of White–Non-White Income Differentials") computed mean incomes from these data for whites and nonwhites by region, age, and education class. The average, marginal, and adjusted MDC's are all defined and discussed in the text.

Columns 1-3 of Table 6 measure the average and columns 4 and 5 the marginal *MDC* at various ages in 1939 between white and non-white elementary, high-school, and college graduates, assuming that nonwhites and whites are really equally productive. In the North both marginals tend to be above the corresponding averages, while in the South they are somewhat below at the college level.

These marginal *MDC*'s measure the ratio of the returns from additional schooling to whites and nonwhites,[54] and are greater, equal to, or less than zero as the return to whites is greater, equal to, or less than that to nonwhites. The previous discussion indicated that the return from college is lower for nonwhites partly because both their costs and their incremental benefits are lower. To the extent that returns differ because of cost differences, they do not measure market discrimination alone; rather they measure the combined effects of market and nonmarket discrimination.

The more general definition in equation (36) tries to correct for these influences by subtracting from the observed differentials those differences that would exist were there no marginal market discrimination. The empirical implementation of such a correction is always difficult;[55] a simple approach is to assume that if there were no marginal market discrimination, whites and nonwhites would receive the same rate of return on their additional schooling. Their respective costs are taken as given, although in reality they may differ because of nonmarket discrimination and other factors.[56] With this approach,

---

[54] According to equation (37), the marginal *MDC* at a particular age would be

$$MDC_{ij} = \frac{\pi_{wj} - \pi_{wi}}{\pi_{nj} - \pi_{ni}} - 1,$$

$$= \frac{\Delta\pi_{wij}}{\Delta\pi_{nij}} - 1,$$

where π_{wi} and π_{wj} are the incomes of whites at two schooling levels, and π_{ni} and π_{nj} are the incomes of nonwhites. But $\Delta\pi_{wij}$ and $\Delta\pi_{nij}$ are simply the returns to whites and nonwhites, respectively, from going from the *i*th to the *j*th school level.

[55] See *ibid.*, pp. 93-95 and 130-131.

[56] One such factor is market discrimination at lower age and educational levels since the lower foregone earnings of nonwhite college students results partly from market discrimination against nonwhite elementary and high-school graduates. Consequently, this approach implies that market discrimination at lower levels reduces the earnings that nonwhite college graduates would receive even if there were no discrimination against nonwhite *college graduates*. This implication may or may not be considered reasonable, but for my purposes it is not necessary to use a more sophisticated method.

the marginal *MDC* becomes proportional to the percentage difference in rates of return, the factor of proportionality being the ratio of costs.[57] So the rate of return and market discrimination approaches come more or less to the same thing when a distinction is drawn between marginal and average discrimination.

Consequently, since the rate of return to nonwhite college graduates is much higher in the South than in the North, the adjusted marginal *MDC* should be much lower there.[58] Moreover, the rather small difference between the rate of return to whites and to southern nonwhites implies that the adjusted *MDC* in the South should be quite small, certainly much smaller than the average and the unadjusted marginal *MDC*'s against college graduates. Column 6 (of Table 6), which assumes that nonwhite college graduates would have received the same rate of return as white graduates were there no market discrimination against them, supports these implications: the adjusted marginal *MDC* is only about .6 in the South compared to 1.4 in the North and to average and unadjusted marginal *MDC*'s in the South of 1.5 and 1.2, respectively.

Market discrimination against southern nonwhite college graduates is apparently relatively small, even though market discrimination

[57] The marginal discrimination coefficient can be written as

$$MDC_{ij} = \frac{\Delta \pi_w}{\Delta \pi_n} - \frac{\Delta \pi_w^0}{\Delta \pi_n^0}.$$

To a first approximation

$$\Delta \pi_w = r_w C_w \text{ and } \Delta \pi_n = r_n C_n,$$

where r_w and r_n are the rates of return and C_w and C_n are the costs of moving from the *i*th to the *j*th educational level. By assumption,

$$\Delta \pi_w^0 = r C_w \text{ and } \Delta \pi_n^0 = r C_n.$$

Therefore, the first equation in the footnote can be written as

$$MDC_{ij} = \frac{r_w C_w}{r_n C_n} - \frac{r C_w}{r C_n}$$

$$= \frac{C_w}{C_n} \left(\frac{r_w - r_n}{r_n} \right).$$

[58] This conclusion presupposes that the rate of return to white college graduates is also not much higher in the South. The available evidence suggests that the rate of return to whites is somewhat higher in the South.

against nonwhites is generally quite large in the South.[59] One possible line of explanation emphasizes that nonwhite college graduates partially avoid white discrimination by catering to their own market, where the discrimination against them is presumably less severe. A relatively large fraction of nonwhite college graduates were, indeed, in occupations that cater to a segregated market: in 1940 about 50 per cent of nonwhite graduates were doctors, dentists, clergymen, teachers, or lawyers, while only 35 per cent of white graduates were.[60] The opportunities to cater to a segregated market were probably more available to southern graduates since the nonwhite market is both larger (relative to supply) and more segregated there.[61] Fewer opportunities to avoid discrimination are available to nonwhite high-school graduates: the same fraction of whites and nonwhites were in occupations not catering to segregated markets.[62] This would explain why column 7 of Table 6, which presents adjusted marginal *MDC*'s against nonwhite high-school graduates, shows substantially greater discrimination in the South.

Let me emphasize, however, in concluding this section, that a much more intensive examination of the evidence, especially of that collected in the 1960 Census, is necessary before these findings can be fully accepted.

WOMEN

Absolute income differentials are much smaller for female than male college graduates, but the rate of return may not be smaller because direct costs are somewhat lower and opportunity costs are much lower

---

[59] The 1950 Census also shows larger earning differentials between college and high-school nonwhites in the South than North (see C. A. Anderson, "Regional and Racial Differences in Relations between Income and Education," *The School Review*, January 1955, pp. 38-46). The 1950 Census data, however, did not separate rural from urban persons, and many more southern than northern nonwhites live in rural areas, especially at lower educational levels. Perhaps this explains why the 1950 Census, unlike the 1940 Census, also shows larger differentials in the South between nonwhites with high-school and elementary school educations.

[60] See *1940 Census of Population, Occupational Characteristics* (sample statistics), Bureau of the Census, Washington, 1943, Table 3.

[61] For a discussion of evidence on income distributions that led to the same interpretation, see Milton Friedman, *A Theory of the Consumption Function*, Princeton for NBER, 1957, pp. 84-85.

[62] For example, in 1940 about 37 per cent of both white and nonwhite high-school graduates were craftsmen, operators, or laborers, occupational groups which do not sell their services to segregated markets. (See *1940 Census of Population, Occupational Characteristics*, Table 3.)

for women. One reason why a smaller money—not necessarily real—rate of return would be expected is the much lower labor force participation of women. In fact, the difference in costs does not seem to compensate fully for the difference in returns. Both Mincer and Renshaw find that the rate of return received by white women college graduates is several percentage points lower than that received by white men.[63] Actual behavior is consistent with the evidence on gains: about 30 per cent of women high-school graduates go to college, while 40 per cent of the men do.[64] Although this difference can also be explained by other factors, such as a prejudice against higher education for women, the fact that a larger fraction of nonwhite than white women high-school graduates have gone to college[65] cannot be so easily explained by these factors since nonwhite women have less resources, are discriminated against even more by certain colleges, etc. Yet nonwhite women might have gained more from college if only because they participate more in the labor force. Indeed, Renshaw does find a high rate of return to nonwhite women college graduates.[66]

Many women drop out of college after marriage, and college women are more likely to marry educated and wealthy men. These well-known facts suggest that women go to college partly to increase the probability of marrying a more desirable man. If the marriage factor were important, the gain to women from additional schooling should be determined by *family* earnings classified by the wife's education rather than by personal earnings so classified,[67] and the full money

[63] See Mincer in *Investment in Human Beings*, p. 68, and Renshaw in *Review of Economics and Statistics*, August 1960.

[64] See *Population Characteristics, Educational Attainment: March 1957*, Tables B and 2, for data referring to 1950 and 1957.

[65] *Ibid.*, Tables C, 2, and 3.

[66] *Review of Economics and Statistics*, August 1960, p. 322.

[67] Presumably the differential in their wives' earnings should be included as part of the gain to men from additional schooling, but double counting would occur if the earnings of both spouses were fully included as gains of both. Probably the ideal way to avoid duplication would be to define returns as

$$R_m = W_1 r_{mm} + W_2 r_{mw}$$
$$R_w = W_1' r_{wm} + W'_2 r_{ww},$$

where R is the full return, the W's are weights, r_{mm} is the differential earnings of men from additional schooling, r_{mw} is the differential earnings of their wives, and r_{wm} and r_{ww} are similar concepts applied to women (very likely $W_1 > W_2$ and $W_2' > W_1'$).

gain to women may be much higher than previous estimates have indicated.

Table 7 presents data from a survey of subscribers to Consumers' Union that classified family income by the education of both spouses.[68] Women college graduates tend to have slightly higher family incomes than men with the same education, while women high-school graduates have much higher family incomes than men high-school graduates.[69] Thus differentials between the family incomes of college and high-school graduates are also much less for women than men. Accordingly, even when the gain from a more lucrative marriage is included, the money rate of return from college seems less for women, a conclusion which is, as already mentioned, consistent with actual behavior. Table 7 suggests that the gain from postgraduate study is also less for women, a result consistent with crude evidence on actual behavior,[70] but perhaps not with evidence restricted to unmarried college graduates.

TABLE 7

FAMILY INCOMES OF MARRIED MEN AND WOMEN IN 1960, BY EDUCATION
AND YEARS AFTER FIRST JOB
(dollars)

Years After First Job	Years of Education and Sex					
	16+ Men (1)	16+ Women (2)	16 Men (3)	16 Women (4)	12 Men (5)	12 Women (6)
7-8	10,140	9,718	8,310	9,190	5,850	7,980
9-10	10,210	10,784	8,920	9,380	6,630	7,410
19-20	11,330	11,018	10,000	10,980	7,470	9,200

Source: May 1960 Survey of subscribers to Consumers' Union sponsored by the Workshop in Expectational Economics of Columbia University.

[68] The survey was conducted by the Workshop in Expectational Economics at Columbia University and I am indebted to Albert Hart and Marshall Kolin for making the data available to me.

[69] Presumably the main reason is that they tend to marry men of higher education, although the high-school figures may also be biased because the relatively small number of male subscribers who never completed high school are included with the male high-school graduates.

[70] See *Population Characteristics, Educational Attainment: March 1957*, Table D.

RURAL PERSONS

Income differentials between college and high-school graduates are apparently much less for rural than for urban persons,[71] but indirect costs are also less[72] because rural high-school graduates earn less than urban ones. They may also be less because rural persons earn relatively more while in college, for they can help with farm chores during summer vacations.[73]

Instead of trying to determine directly whether the differences in returns exceed those in costs, the evidence provided by actual behavior is utilized. A much smaller fraction of the graduates of rural than of urban high schools go to college; indeed, a smaller fraction of rural males go than urban females or urban males with fathers who are manual or service workers. Relatively few rural graduates go to college even when family income, I.Q., type of high-school curriculum, scholastic standing, and several other variables are held constant.[74] The difference in returns is apparently more important than the difference in costs.

[71] See *Income of Families and Persons in the United States* for 1956 and 1958, Current Population Report, Series P-60, Nos. 27 and 33, U.S. Bureau of the Census, Washington, 1958 and 1960, and other calculations from Census data included in an unpublished manuscript by Z. Griliches.

[72] It is not clear whether direct costs are less. On the one hand, tuition is less because rural persons more frequently attend heavily subsidized state colleges; on the other hand, transportation and other direct costs are higher because they attend colleges further from their homes than urban persons do.

[73] In October 1960 students ages 18-24 worked a slightly smaller number of hours relative to nonstudents of the same age when employed in agriculture than when employed elsewhere. (See *The Employment of Students, October 1960*, Bureau of Labor Statistics, Special Labor Force Report, No. 16, Washington, 1961, Tables E and F.) I suspect, however, that summer employment is much greater for rural college students, so that on balance they forego relatively less earnings. This has certainly been true at the high-school level, where rural students work more than urban ones during the school year (see, e.g., *ibid.*), and even attend school many fewer days.

Indeed, the much heralded increase in the length of the school year since the turn of the century has been entirely the result of the spread to rural areas of patterns already established sixty years ago in New York, Chicago, and other large cities (see E. Denison "The Residual Factor and Economic Growth," paper prepared for a May 1963 meeting of the OECD). One might even claim that the recent development of trimester and quarterly systems at many colleges and a few high schools is a reaction to the secular growth of foregone earnings and the spread of urbanization. Since urban communities do not experience the summer increase in demand for labor that rural ones do, the summer holiday is an anachronism and an expensive luxury in a high-wage urban community.

[74] See *Factors Related to College Attendance of Farm and Nonfarm High School Graduates: 1960*, Tables 11, 12, 15, and 16.

4. *Variation in Rates of Return*

The private rate of return to cohorts of white male college graduates seems considerable even after adjustment for differential ability. Rates to cohorts of college drop-outs, nonwhites, women, and rural persons, although smaller, are also far from negligible. Evidence such as this has encouraged various public bodies and interested citizens to exhort young persons in their own interest to go to college and to succeed in graduating. Now results for cohorts can be applied to individuals only if different members of a cohort are affected more or less to the same extent; if, however, they are affected very differently, they may well be justified in largely ignoring the cohort results.

The gain from college has been shown to vary by sex, race, urban or rural, and graduate or drop-out status, and (see section 2) even within a given demographic group, according to ability. This section indicates that the variation in gain within a group like white male college graduates is much greater than can even be explained by the variation in ability alone. So great is it that an individual can be only loosely guided by the gain of his cohort, and has to place considerable weight on his own situation and hope for the best.

Table 8 presents, for several age classes and high-school and college graduates, coefficients of variation in the incomes of native-white

TABLE 8

COEFFICIENTS OF VARIATION IN AFTER-TAX INCOME OF WHITE MALES,
BY AGE AND YEARS OF EDUCATION, 1939 AND 1949

	1949		1939	
Age	12 (1)	16+ (2)	12 (3)	16+ (4)
25–29	.44	.75	.55	.73
30–34	.47	.59	.69	.75
35–44	.60	.75	.79	.66
45–54	.83	1.01	.75	.66
55–64	1.05	.92	.77	.68

Source: Computed from 1940 Census of Population, Education, and 1950 Census of Population, Education. The 1949 incomes apply to all white males, while those for 1939 apply only to urban native-white males. The adjustments for personal income taxes are described in Appendix A.

urban males in 1939 and white males in 1949.[75] The variation is certainly not negligible since these coefficients average more than two-thirds. There is some tendency, especially in 1949, for the variation to increase with age,[76] while there is little systematic difference by educational level.

These coefficients do not fully measure the variation in income among all members of a given educational cohort because only the incomes of survivors are included and, therefore, the dispersion in length of life is ignored. The latter is still considerable, although it has declined over time along with the decline in mortality.[77]

Columns 1 and 2 of Table 9 present coefficients of variation in survivorship from 18 to selected ages.[78] These are larger at older ages and smaller in 1949 than in 1939.

[75] Similar measures for 1949 can be found in H. Houthakker, *Review of Economics and Statistics,* February 1959, Table 1. I shall only consider the dispersion among white males, although it would be of some interest to compare different races and sexes.

[76] Some of the increase is spurious because the two youngest age classes cover only five years while the three oldest cover ten. The variation is generally larger, the larger the number of years covered by an age class because earnings tend either to rise or decline systematically with age.

The 16+ category in 1939 failed to show a rise with age almost certainly because independent professionals were not included in these calculations. Their dispersion definitely rises with age and they would be more important at older ages. The inclusion of property income in 1949 and the exclusion of self-employed persons in 1939 explains why the variation seems to be lower in 1939, especially at older ages and among college graduates.

[77] In the United States the expected lifespan (ignoring years after age 65) of eighteen-year-old males increased from 32 years in 1900 to 38 years in 1950, while the coefficient of variation changed even more, from 0.74 to 0.54. (For 1900, see *United States Life Tables 1890, 1901, 1910 and 1901-1910,* Bureau of the Census, Washington, 1921, Table 3. For 1950, see *United States Life Tables 1949-51,* Vital Statistics-Special Reports, National Office of Vital Statistics, Vol. 41, No. 1, Washington 1954, Table 2.)

A revealing comment on the dispersion in length of life in the past was made by Adam Smith: "The work which he learns to perform . . . will replace to him the whole expense of his education, with at least the ordinary profits of any equally valuable capital. It must do this too in a reasonable time, *regard being had to the very uncertain duration of human life, in the same manner as to the more certain duration of the machine." (Wealth of Nations,* New York, 1937, Book I, Chapter X, my italics.)

[78] If a random variable S_x takes on the value of 1 when a person survives from age 18 to age x, and the value of 0 when he dies before x, the square of the coefficient of variation of S_x equals

$$G(S_x) = \frac{1 - P_x}{P_x},$$

where P_x is the probability of surviving to age x and, therefore, also the expected value of S_x. Columns 1 and 2 list different values of $[G(S_x)]^{1/2}$.

TABLE 9

COEFFICIENTS OF VARIATION IN MORTALITY AND COHORT INCOMES FOR
COLLEGE AND HIGH-SCHOOL GRADUATES, BY AGE, 1939 AND 1949

Age	Coefficient of Variation in Mortality		Coefficient of Variation in Income by Years of Education			
			1939		1949	
	1939	1949	12	16+	12	16+
	(1)	(2)	(3)	(4)	(5)	(6)
25–29	.14	.12	.57	.75	.46	.77
30–34	.18	.16	.72	.79	.50	.62
35–44	.26	.22	.85	.72	.65	.79
45–54	.39	.34	.89	.81	.94	1.12
55–64	.61	.55	1.09	1.01	1.31	1.18

Source: Cols. 1-2 computed from State and Regional Life
Tables 1939–41, and United States Life Tables 1949–51; cols. 3-6
computed from cols. 1 and 2 and from Table 8, using the formula
in footnote 80.

A more complete measure of variation within a cohort would take account of both survivorship and the incomes of survivors, and such measures are shown in the rest of Table 9.[79] At younger ages the full variation is not much greater than that in incomes alone because the probability of surviving to these ages is close to unity. But at older ages it is significantly greater—more than a third greater at ages 55-64 —because the variation in survivorship becomes quite large then. The substantial increase in the variation of survivorship with age makes the full variation increase rather sharply with age, generally being more than 50 per cent larger at ages 55-64 than at 25-29. There is still

[79] The problem is to find the coefficient of variation in $S_x I_x$, where S_x is defined in the previous footnote and I_x measures incomes at age x. Since S_x takes on the value of 1 for survivors and 0 for others, the relevant income variable is that of survivors. If I_x is so defined, the variance of SI is

$$\sigma^2(SI) = (1 - P) P^2 (EI)^2 + P[EI^2 - 2P(EI)^2 + P^2(EI)^2]$$
$$= P[EI^2 - P(EI)^2]$$
$$= P[\sigma^2(I) + (EI)^2 (1 - P)]$$
$$= P \sigma^2(I) + \sigma^2(S) (EI)^2$$

and

$$G(SI) = \frac{\sigma^2(SI)}{(ESI)^2} = \frac{G(I)}{P} + G(S).$$

These equations also follow as special cases of recent theorems on the variation of products if the distribution of I defined over all values of S was independent of the distribution of S. (See L. A. Goodman, "On the Exact Variance of Products," *Journal of the American Statistical Association,* December 1960.) In other words, the distribution of I among survivors would be the same as the full distribution of I.

no appreciable relation with education, although the variation among college graduates is usually greater in 1949.

Although these adjusted coefficients are interesting and relevant, they would be the appropriate measures of the variation within co-horts only if different educational levels were mutually exclusive alternatives, as working in New York or San Francisco are. A college graduate is, however, usually also a high-school and elementary-school graduate. Therefore, a person deciding whether to go to college wants to know how much *additional* variation is caused by going, in the same way that nonwhites want to know how much additional dis-crimination results from moving to a higher educational level. In other words, the additional or marginal variation caused by a college education should be measured, just as the marginal discrimination against nonwhite college graduates was measured (see section 3).

If the gain from college is measured by the rate of return, marginal variation should be measured by the variation in this rate. According to the analysis in Chapter III, if returns were the same in each year and lasted forever, the rate of return could be written as

$$r = k/C,$$

where r is the rate, k is the return in any year, and C is the cost of college. The variation in r would be larger, the larger the variation in k and C and the smaller the correlation between them.[80] If returns were not the same in different years, the simple formula in equation (38) would not hold, but it is apparent that the variation in r would be smaller, the smaller the serial correlation among returns.

Therefore, the variation in the rate of return among members of a given cohort depends on four basic parameters: the variation in costs, the variation in returns, the correlation between returns and costs, and the correlation between returns in different periods.[81] Unfortu-nately, little is known about some of these, so the effect of college on

[80] If σ^2 stands for the variance and E for the expected value,

$$\sigma^2(r) = E^2(k)\,\sigma^2\left(\frac{1}{C}\right) + E^2\left(\frac{1}{C}\right)\sigma^2(k) + \sigma(k)\,\sigma\left(\frac{1}{C}\right),$$

when the correlation between k and $\frac{1}{C}$ equals zero. A more complicated formula applies when it differs from zero (see *ibid.*).

[81] Both these correlations are special cases of the more general correlation between income differentials (either costs or returns) in different periods.

income variation cannot yet be fully ascertained. But I shall try to determine what the effect appears to be by briefly discussing what is known about each parameter.

Least is known about the correlation between costs and returns. The significant differences between the incomes of graduates from Negro and other cheaper colleges and those from Ivy League and other expensive ones[82] certainly indicate that the correlation is positive. The fact, however, that graduates of the same college receive very different incomes suggests that although the correlation may be positive and significant, it is also very far from perfect.[83]

The variation in costs among college graduates is apparently considerable. For in 1940 the coefficient of variation in expenditures per student in one state alone—New York—was .9 among private colleges and .3 among public ones,[84] and the variation in the whole country was surely greater. Moreover, I have already shown that foregone earnings can vary widely, certainly among demographic groups, and probably also within groups, because of differences in ability, local labor market conditions, and so forth.

There is no direct evidence on the serial correlation of returns to college graduates, but it probably can be closely approximated by a weighted average of the serial correlation between the incomes of college graduates and of high-school graduates.[85] The correlation be-

---

[82] Some evidence on the incomes of graduates from different schools can be found in E. Havemann and P. S. West, *They Went to College*, New York, 1952. Their book is based on the survey of incomes in 1947 by Time Magazine. As mentioned in section 2, Hunt ("Income Determinants for College Graduates") used the same data and found a positive relation between the incomes of alumni and estimates of the amount spent on students by different colleges.

[83] Thus the partial regression coefficient that Hunt finds between incomes and expenditures, although sizable, is just barely statistically significant.

[84] Computed from "Statistics of Higher Education, 1939-40," Chapter IV, Tables 18 and 19.

[85] If $k_1 = \Upsilon_{c1} - \Upsilon_{h1}$ and $k_0 = \Upsilon_{c0} - \Upsilon_{h0}$ were the returns in years 1 and 0, respectively, the correlation coefficient between returns would be

$$R(k_0, k_1) = \frac{\text{Cov }(k_0, k_1)}{\sigma(k_0)\ \sigma(k_1)}.$$

If Υ_c and Υ_h were always uncorrelated, and if small y's represent deviations from means,

$$\text{Cov }(k_0, k_1) = E\ (y_{c1} - y_{h1})\ (y_{c0} - y_{h0})$$
$$= E\ (y_{c1}y_{c0}) + E\ (y_{h1}\ y_{h0}),$$

and

$$\sigma^2(k) = E\ (y_c - y_h)^2 = \sigma^2(y_c) + \sigma^2(y_h).$$

tween the adjacent incomes of persons with a given education is very high and even those between incomes separated by a few years remain high.[86] While the correlation between incomes separated by many years is probably much less, one explanation may be that these inter-mingle a positive correlation between returns in different periods and a positive correlation between returns and costs.[87]

Remaining is the variation in returns during any period, which depends on the variation in the earnings of college graduates (given for white males in Table 9), the variation in their earnings if they had not gone on to college, and the correlation between these two. The variation in the earnings of college graduates if they had not gone to college may differ from the actual variation among high-school

---

Then

$$R\ (k_0, k_1) = \frac{E\ (y_{c1}\ y_{c0}) + E\ (y_{h1}\ y_{h0})}{[\sigma^2(y_{c1}) + \sigma^2(y_{h1})]\ [\sigma^2(y_{c0}) + \sigma^2(y_{h0})].}$$

If it is assumed for simplicity that

$$\sigma^2(y_{c1}) = \sigma^2(y_{c0}) = \sigma^2(y_c), \text{ and } \sigma^2(y_{h1}) = \sigma^2(y_{h0}) = \sigma^2(y_h),$$

then

$$R(k_0, k_1) = R\ (y_{c1}, y_{c0}) \frac{\sigma^2(y_c)}{\sigma^2(y_c) + \sigma^2(y_h)} + R\ (y_{h1}, y_{h0}) \frac{\sigma^2(y_h)}{\sigma^2(y_c) + \sigma^2(y_h)}$$

$$= wR\ (y_{c1}, y_{c0}) + (1 - w)R\ (y_{h1}, y_{h0}).$$

The major assumption is that Y_c and Y_h are uncorrelated, but the result would not be very different if they were positively correlated. For the correlation between returns would be greater, equal to, or less than that given in the last equation as

$$R\ (y_{ct'}\ y_{ht'}) \gtreqless R\ (y_{ct}, y_{ht})\ R\ (y_{et}, y_{et'}),$$

where the left term is the average correlation coefficient between the incomes of college graduates in year t and otherwise equivalent high-school graduates in t'; the first term on the right is the average correlation coefficient between their incomes in the same year; and the second term on the right is the average correlation coefficient between the incomes in t and t' of persons with the same education. If the forces determining $R\ (Y_{ct'}\ Y_{ht})$ were independent of those determining $R\ (y_{et}, y_{et'})$, as is probably approximately true, equality would hold, and the correlation between returns would be given by the equation above.

86 Some correlations for independent professionals, whose earnings are presumably less stable than those of the typical college graduate, averaged about .85 between adjacent earnings and .75 between those separated by two years (see Friedman, *Consumption Function*, Table 18; for other evidence see, I. Kravis, *The Structure of Income*, Philadelphia, 1962, Chapter VIII).

87 See Mincer in *Investment in Human Beings*, p. 53, especially footnote 8.

graduates because of the differences in "ability" between college and high-school graduates discussed in section 2. As pointed out there, however, three important measures of "ability"—rank in class, I.Q., and father's occupation—although they have significant effects on the earnings of college graduates, apparently have little effect on those of high-school graduates. If they are representative of the effects of other differences, the actual variation in high-school earnings could be used to estimate the hypothetical variation among college graduates. The same argument suggests that the correlation between these earnings would not be very high, for the factors making earnings high among college graduates are apparently quite different from those making them high among high-school graduates.

TABLE 10

COEFFICIENTS OF VARIATION IN THE RETURNS TO COLLEGE GRADUATES, BY AGE, 1939 AND 1949[a]

Age	1939 (1)	1949 (2)
25-29	3.35	8.73
	1.28	3.57
30-34	2.74	1.72
	.91	.94
35-44	2.56	2.00
	.47	1.00
45-54	2.59	2.55
	.65	1.33
55-64	3.09	2.98
	.84	.99

Source: Table 9 and the formula $\sigma^2(R) = \sigma^2(c) + \sigma^2(h) - 2r_{ch}\sigma(c)\sigma(h)$, where R is the return, and c and h represent the earnings of college and high-school graduates, and σ^2 represents a variance.

[a] Top entries assume that incomes of college and high-school graduates are uncorrelated aside from mortality experience; bottom entries assume that they are perfectly correlated.

Table 10 presents estimates of the coefficient of variation in the return to college graduates. These assume that the variation in the income of college graduates if they had not gone to college can be measured by the actual variation among high-school graduates. Two estimates are presented at each age class: one assuming no correlation between the incomes of college and high-school graduates aside from a common mortality experience,[88] and the other assuming a perfect correlation. As already mentioned, the true correlation is a good deal closer to the first. The table indicates a very substantial coefficient of variation in the returns to college graduates, probably averaging over 2.0. As opposed to the variation in income (see Table 9), there is no systematic tendency for this variation to increase with age.

Let us now bring together the discussion of these four parameters. The coefficient of variation in returns is very large, probably averaging more than 2.0. The variation in costs is also large, although not as large as that in returns, and costs and returns are positively correlated. Consequently, the variation in returns per dollar of cost, equation (5), is probably lower, but not very much lower, than that in returns alone. Since returns are not perfectly correlated over time, the variation in the rate of return is less than that in returns per dollar of cost. The difference is not great, however, since the correlation of returns over time is apparently very high. The net effect would seem to be a rather high variation in the rate of return; the coefficient of variation is almost certainly higher than one and possibly a good deal so.

One way to illustrate the magnitude of the variation is to point out that although a cohort of white males might receive a private rate of return of 12 per cent, many members will receive more than 25 or less than 0 per cent.[89] The existence of many low and even negative returns has been presumed by others from the wide overlapping of the distributions of the earning of college and high-school graduates.

[88] The correlation coefficient between the incomes of college and high-school graduates at a particular age x equals

$$r = \frac{E\left[(S_{cx}I_{cx} - ES_{cx}EI_{cx})(S_{hx}I_{hx} - ES_{hx}EI_{hx})\right]}{E(S_{cx}I_{cx})\,E(S_{hx}I_{hx})\,\sqrt{G(S_{cx}I_{cx})\,G(S_{hx}I_{hx})}},$$

where S, G, etc., are defined in previous footnotes. Now if $S_c = S_h = S_x$ and if I_c and I_h are uncorrelated, then

$$E\left[(S\,I_c - ES\,EI_c)(SI_h\,EI_h)\right] = ES^2EI_cEI_h - (ES)^2EI_cEI_h = EI_cEI_h\,\sigma^2(S),$$

and therefore

$$r_{min} = \frac{G(S)}{\sqrt{G(SI_c)\,G(SI_h)}}$$

[89] If rates of return were normally distributed and if the coefficient of variation equaled one, about one-third of the members would receive rates either above 24 or below 0 per cent.

Another way is to compare it with the variation in the rate of return to physical capital. Many persons have stressed that a dynamic competitive economy produces considerable variation in the gain from capital and some rough estimates by Stigler confirm this: the coefficient of variation in the returns per dollar of capital invested in a group of smaller corporate manufacturing firms was somewhere between one and two.[90] About the same variation was found in the return per dollar invested in a college education. But since the stability of the returns to education is apparently much greater,[91] the variation in rates of return on college education is very likely greater than that on manufacturing capital in smaller corporate firms.

A final question to be discussed is: How much of this large variation in the gain from a college education can be anticipated due to known differences in ability, environment, etc., and, therefore, should not be considered part of the *ex ante* risk? I have already argued that differences in gain due to race, sex, or urban-rural status should not be considered risk since they are, at least in part, anticipated and thus affect behavior. One factor making it easy to anticipate differences even within a demographic group is the unusual stability of returns. On the other hand, differences in known measures of ability, like I.Q. and grades, are small,[92] and have a rather small effect on earning (see section 2). Moreover, investors in education are much younger than investors in business capital; college students are generally in their early twenties, and are certainly not yet fully aware of their talents.

An important factor increasing the difficulty of anticipating the gain from college is that it is collected over a very long time. While business investments are often said to pay off within five or ten years, the pay-off from college takes much longer: the unadjusted rate of return to the 1949 cohort of white male graduates is about 13 per cent; yet ten years after graduation it would still be negative and after a full fifteen years only about 6 per cent. A long pay-off period increases risk along with low correlations between returns by reducing the value of information available when investing. Incidentally, the

[90] See G. J. Stigler, *Capital and Rates of Return in Manufacturing Industries*, Princeton for NBER, 1963, p. 63, footnote 14.

[91] Stigler found a correlation of only .7 between the adjacent, and much smaller correlations between the nonadjacent, average returns per dollar of capital in different manufacturing industries (*ibid.*, Table 18). Presumably the ranking among firms is even less stable.

[92] For example, the coefficient of variation in the I.Q. of college graduates is only 13 per cent (computed from Wolfle, *America's Resources*, Table G-2).

long pay-off period increases the advantage of an education that is useful in many kinds of future economic environments. If "liberal" education were identified with such flexible education, as well it may be, there would be an important economic argument for liberal education, as well as arguments based on intellectual and cultural considerations.

CHAPTER V

Underinvestment in College Education?

THIS chapter adds several dimensions to the evaluation of the effects of college education on earnings and productivity by comparing private and social gains from college education with those from other investments. These comparisons permit a determination of how much is gained or lost by individuals and society from investing in the former rather than the latter, and are essential to determine whether there is underinvestment in college education; they also help determine whether the capital market difficulties, the lack of knowledge and liquidity, etc., outlined in Chapter III (see section 2) have been serious impediments to the flow of resources into college education.

1. Private Money Gains

In discussing whether the private gain from college exceeds that on other investments, a distinction must be made between the typical college graduate and the typical high-school graduate. Chapter IV indicated that the former gains more from college than the latter would, that he comes from a much higher socioeconomic background (see Table 4), and that he very likely finances his education with resources that would otherwise (in part at least) have been invested elsewhere, while the latter often would have to borrow, live frugally as a student, or work overtime (after school). For the sake of brevity, the discussion is limited to white male graduates, although interesting comparisons could be made with drop-outs, nonwhites, and women.

The private rate of return after adjusting for differential "ability" seems to be more than 12 per cent to the cohort of white male college graduates. When comparing the rate on college with rates that would have been obtained if the resources spent on college had been invested elsewhere, there has been a rather surprising tendency to select rates on liquid investments bearing little risk, such as government bonds or savings accounts.[1] The discussion has just indicated (Chapter IV, section 4), however, that an investment in college education is subject to considerable risk, and is obviously extremely illiquid. Consequently, the gain from education should be compared with that on investments with equally large risk and illiquidity.

The earlier analysis indicated that the variation in the rate of return from corporate manufacturing investments is of the same general order of magnitude as that from college education. Stigler estimated the average rate of return on the former at a little over 7 per cent,[2] several percentage points higher than that on riskless assets, but still much lower than the 12+ per cent received by white male college graduates. Although this difference of some 5 percentage points might be explained by compensating differences in liquidity and taxation,[3] a more reasonable inference would be that the private money gain from college to the typical white male graduate is greater than what could have been obtained by investing elsewhere.

An estimate of the money gain could be found by discounting the adjusted income differentials between college and high-school graduates at a rate measuring alternative opportunities. If the 4 per cent riskless rate were used, the present value[4] of the gain to the 1949 cohort of white males would be more than $30,000; the more appropriate rate of 6 per cent would cut the gain to under $20,000, and the possibly still more appropriate rate of 10 per cent would cut it to under $4,000. Although all these estimates are very much under the

---

[1] See P. C. Glick and H. P. Miller, "Educational Level and Potential Income," *American Sociological Review*, June 1956, p. 310; and J. Morgan and M. H. David, "Education and Income," *Quarterly Journal of Economics*, August 1963, p. 435.

[2] G. J. Stigler, *Capital and Rates of Return in Manufacturing Industries*, Princeton for NBER, 1963, Table 10.

For each year from 1938-57, a rate of return was defined for all corporate manufacturing firms as the ratio of after-tax profits to total capital. The simple average of these ratios equals about 7 per cent both during 1938-47 and 1947-57.

[3] Investors in firms could sometimes avoid the high personal income tax by converting ordinary income into capital gains; investors in education cannot. The fact that depreciation on physical capital can be explicitly deducted from taxable income while that on education cannot, at first glance, also seems to favor investment in firms. A closer look, however, raises some serious doubts (see Chapter II, section 1, and Chapter VII, section 2).

[4] By "present value" is meant the value at the time of entrance into college.

$100,000 figure often bandied about,[5] they are not insignificant. For example, even if the gain were "only" $3,500 (a 10 per cent rate), average tuition and fees in 1949 could have been raised by more than 300 per cent without wiping it out.[6]

The typical high-school graduate is another story. Instead of more than 12 per cent, he would receive 10-11 per cent if he went to college. Moreover, instead of investing resources that could have been invested elsewhere he would have to finance much of his college education by borrowing from friends or relatives,[7] by living frugally, or by working after school and during vacations. Since households regularly pay from 8 to 18 per cent on bank and instalment credit loans and even more on others, the cost of borrowing and/or the preference for present consumption must be considered substantial. Consequently, even an 11 per cent rate of return from college would not bulk very large, especially when it is recognized that liquidity considerations would be important here because these persons presumably have a limited command of liquid assets.[8]

So while a college education seems to yield a net money gain to the typical white male college graduate, it may not to the typical white male high-school graduate. One should note, however, that the rapid growth in recent years of low-interest student loans subsidized by state and federal governments[9] certainly must increase the attractiveness of a college education. A study of the demand for these loans should shed considerable light on the conclusions reached here, and

[5] Derived by Glick and Miller, *American Sociological Review*, June 1956. For a critical comment on their estimate, see H. O. Houthakker, "Education and Income," *Review of Economics and Statistics*, February 1959, pp. 27-28.

[6] Tuition and fees are estimated at $230 per student per year in 1949 (see Appendix A, section 2b). They could have been raised to over $1,000 without wiping out the gain.

[7] Or in recent years from governments. See later discussion.

[8] Thus, according to one study, lack of money is the major reason given for not going to college by high-school seniors from lower-income families, while it is a relatively minor reason given by seniors from higher-income families (see *Educational Status, College Plans, and Occupational Status of Farm and Nonfarm Youths: October 1959*, U.S. Bureau of Census, Series ERS (P-27), No. 30, Washington, 1961, Table D).

[9] As of September 1963, New York State alone had more than $72 million outstanding in loans (see *The New York Times*, Sept. 22, 1963). By mid-1960 the National Defense Student Loan Fund amounted to almost $80 million (see A. Rivlin, *The Role of the Federal Government in Financing Higher Education*, Washington, 1961, p. 77).

especially on the capital market impediments to investment in college education.[10]

2. *Social Productivity Gains*

The social economic gain from education, the gain to society as opposed to individuals, could differ from the private gain because of differences between social and private costs and returns. Economists (and others) have generally had little success in estimating the social effects of different investments, and, unfortunately, education is no exception. One can, however, develop some lower and upper limits that effectively rule out many of the more fanciful assertions about the effects of education.

Total social as well as private costs would be the sum of direct and indirect costs. Direct costs are clearly greater to society than to students because some of the expenditures on students are paid out of public and private subsidies. Obviously, "free" state and municipal colleges use scarce resources and are not free to society. Indirect costs, on the other hand, would be greater to society only if the output of students foregone by society exceeded the earnings foregone by students, which is not so obviously true.

Direct social costs would be the sum of educational expenditures by colleges and the social cost of books and additional living expenses. While the latter can be approximated by their private cost, an estimate of educational expenditures is not obtained as easily since colleges spend money on athletic competitions, room and board, adult education, research, medical care, etc., as well as on education proper. In other words, they are multiproduct "firms" with a total expenditure much greater than that on the single product education. I have tried to approximate educational expenditures by eliminating expenditures on "noneducational activities," extension services, research, and "specialized instruction" from the total.[11]

Although social costs should obviously include capital as well as current costs, the fraction of educational expenditures paid by fees

10 Although bearing low-interest rates, these loans are not "easy" in all respects; in particular, they usually require repayment within a much shorter period of time than it takes to collect the pay-off from a college education (on the pay-off period, see section 4 of Chapter IV).

11 For definitions of these terms, see "Statistics of Higher Education, 1955-56," *Biennial Survey of Education in the United States, 1954-1956,* Washington, 1959, Chapter 4, Section II, pp. 58-80. For a further discussion, see Appendix A, section 2c.

has usually been overestimated because only current expenditures have been considered. Since educational institutions are quite capital intensive, expenditures are substantially raised and the fraction attributed to fees lowered when physical capital is included. For example, in 1950 the use value of capital in colleges was about 26 per cent of current expenditures, so that although fees were 42 per cent of current expenditures, they were only about 33 per cent of all expenditures. The full private contribution to all social costs has, however, been greatly underestimated because indirect costs are generally ignored, and they are mostly a private cost. If, for example, foregone earnings were used to represent indirect social costs, college students would be paying through tuition, fees, and foregone earnings almost three-quarters of all social costs.

Social and private economic returns from college would differ if a college education had different effects on earnings and productivity. A student generally needs only determine the effect of a college education on his earnings, but society needs to determine its effect on national income. Thus if college graduates earn more partly because their productivity was systematically overestimated, private returns would tend to be larger than social ones. A more common criticism, however, is that earnings greatly understate the social productivity of college graduates (and other educated persons) because they are (allegedly) only partly compensated for their effect on the development and spread of economic knowledge. In technical language, social returns are said to be larger than private returns because of the external economies produced by college graduates.

As a first approximation, social returns will be measured by the before-tax earnings differentials, tax payments being one kind of external economy, and indirect social costs will be measured by the before-tax earnings foregone. The social rate of return, unadjusted for differential ability, would then be about 13 per cent to the 1939 cohort of urban, native-white, male college graduates and 12.5 per cent to the 1949 cohort of white male college graduates. These are only slightly less than the private rates because differential tax payments almost offset the subsidies to college education. Similar results would be found for drop-outs and for nonwhite, female, and rural college graduates.[12] Adjustments for I.Q., grades, and other ability

12 For example, social rates of return to the 1939 cohorts of urban native-white, male drop-outs and urban, southern, nonwhite, male graduates are estimated at 8.5 and 11 per cent, respectively, compared with private rates of 9 and 11.9 per cent.

factors would have about the same effect on the social rates as they did on the private rates: relatively little for the typical college person, and a few percentage points for the typical high-school graduate (if he had gone to college).

The development of a more sophisticated estimate of the social gain is not easy because other external effects are very difficult to measure. The absence of any direct measurements forced me to use an indirect and not very reliable method. E. Denison has recently estimated the contribution of physical capital, labor, increasing returns, and many other factors to economic growth in the United States. After deducting these contributions, a residual is left over that he calls the contribution of "advancement in knowledge."[13] By attributing all of the residual to education,[14] an upper limit to the social effect of education can be developed.[15]

According to Denison, about .58 percentage points of the 1.60 per cent average annual growth from 1929 to 1957 in national income per person employed is explained by the growth in knowledge,[16] and about .67 percentage points by the growth in education.[17] If the growth in knowledge was considered an indirect effect of the growth in education, the share attributed to education would almost double. This in turn implies that the estimated average rate of return on education would also almost double.[18]

[13] See his *Sources of Economic Growth in the United States*, New York, 1962.

[14] S. G. Strumilin, in an interpretation of economic growth in the Soviet Union, does consider the "residual" to be a "social" effect of education (see his "The Economics of Education in the U.S.S.R.," *International Social Science Journal*, 1962, No. 4, p. 642).

[15] Although a likely upper limit, it is not a necessary one because larger external economies from education might have been nullified by net external diseconomies from other sources.

[16] *Sources of Economic Growth*, Table 33. The amount (residual) attributed to knowledge would be different if different assumptions had been made about the importance of economies of scale, restrictions against the optimal use of resources, etc. For example, if all the increase in output per unit of input resulted from advances in knowledge, the contribution of such advances would rise to .93 percentage points.

[17] *Ibid.* The contribution of education is based on before-tax earning differentials liberally adjusted for ability (*ibid.*, Chap. 7).

[18] The increase in income attributable to an increase in education can be written as:

$$y = k\frac{C}{Y} = kI,$$ where y is the percentage increase in income, k is the effect on income

of investing a dollar in education, and I is the fraction of income invested in education. If the effect of a given investment in education were to double, y and thus k would double. But since $r \rightleftharpoons k$, where r is the rate of return, a doubling of k would approximately double r.

If the contribution of different educational levels to the advance in knowledge were proportionate to their direct effects on earnings— possibly college graduates had a disproportionately large contribution—the unadjusted social rate of return to white male graduates would be estimated at close to 25 per cent. The initial estimate of the social rate, 13 per cent, and the 25 per cent provide a lower and an admittedly rough upper limit to the true rate, the difference between them measuring the ignorance of external effects. Although this difference is embarrassingly large, it does suggest that, contrary to many assertions, the private economic gain from education is much of the social economic gain. For the private gain is more than half of the apparent upper limit, and presumably a good deal more than half of the true social rate.

In recent years the federal government has been subsidizing investment in education through scholarships and loans,[19] and investment in business capital through accelerated depreciation, tax credits, and other means. Somehow the limited funds available must be allocated between these different kinds of investment. One determinant clearly should be, and hopefully is, their relative contribution to national income, a topic which will now be discussed briefly.

A first approximation to the social rate of return on business capital can be found by relating profits to capital, with profits including the corporate income and other direct taxes.[20] The before-tax rate of return on corporate manufacturing capital averaged about 12 per cent for both 1938-47 and 1947-57,[21] compared to an after-tax rate of 7 per cent. If the before-tax rate on all corporations were between 10 and 13 per cent and that on unincorporated firms between 4 and 8 per cent, almost the same as the after-tax rate on corporations, the rate on all business capital would be between 8 and 12 per cent.[22] The first approximation to the social rate of return to white male college graduates would be between 10 and 13 per cent after adjustment for differential ability. Since the rates to drop-outs, women, and nonwhites would be a few percentage points lower, the rate to all

[19] See Rivlin, *Role of Federal Government,* Chapters 4-5.

[20] This method assumes only that direct taxes come *initially* out of the return on capital; it is consistent with any kind of *ultimate* incidence.

[21] Computed by adding the tax payments of corporate manufacturing firms to Stigler's after-tax profits.

[22] About 80 per cent of all tangible business capital seems to be in corporations (computed from Vol. II of *Studies in the National Balance Sheet of the United States* by R. Goldsmith, R. Lipsey, and M. Mendelson, Princeton for NBER, 1963).

college entrants would be between 8 and 11 per cent. The rates on business capital and college education seem, therefore, to fall within the same range.

A fuller treatment of external effects could, however, change the picture entirely. It has been seen that if all the unexplained residual for 1929-57 were attributed to education, its estimated social rate would almost double; if, on the other hand, all was attributed to business capital, its estimated social rate would much more than double.[23] Consequently, depending on the allocation of the residual, i.e., the "advance in knowledge," the estimated social rate on college education could be as much as twice and as little as less than half of that on business capital. Ignorance about the "residual," therefore, precludes at present any firm judgment about the relative social rates on business capital and college education.

3. Private Real Rates

A treatment of the full, as opposed to the economic, social rate of return on college education would involve a consideration of cultural advance, democratic government, etc., and is clearly far beyond the scope of this study. Even a treatment of the full private rate is exceedingly difficult and I shall be content simply to raise some questions and suggest a few very tentative answers.

In deciding whether to go to college, attitudes toward college life and studying, the kind of work college graduates do, and other psychic factors are relevant as well as the gain in earnings. Full or real returns and costs would be the sum of monetary and psychic ones, and the real gain would depend on the relation between these real returns and costs. The psychic gain from college, like the monetary gain, probably differs considerably between the typical college and high-school graduate. For presumably the former does and the latter does not go to college partly because of a difference in expected psychic gains.[24] Or to use more direct evidence, lack of interest is usually a major reason cited by high-school seniors in explaining why they were

---

[23] The effect on the business rate is much greater than that on education because the estimated direct contribution of business capital to growth is much less than that of education (see Denison, *Sources of Economic Growth*, Table 33).

[24] For a similar argument applied to monetary gains, see section 2 of Chapter IV.

not going to college, and by college drop-outs in explaining why they never finished.[25]

Quantitative estimates of psychic gains are never directly available and are usually computed residually as the difference between independent estimates of monetary and real gains.[26] Unfortunately, independent estimates of the real gains to college graduates are not available. For example, they could not be measured by the monetary gains from other capital because there may also be psychic gains from such capital,[27] and, more importantly, because the real gains from college and other capital may differ owing to differences in access to the capital market or to other factors. One can use actual behavior to test whether real gains do differ. For if, say, college education were an unusually attractive investment, pressure would develop to invest more there, and while it could be offset in the short run by financing and other difficulties, these could be at least partially surmounted in the long run.

Table 11 indicates that the gross investment in college education rose from about 2.5 per cent of that in physical capital in 1920 to

TABLE 11

INVESTMENT IN COLLEGE EDUCATION RELATIVE TO PHYSICAL
CAPITAL FOR SELECTED YEARS

	Ratio of Investment in College to Gross Physical Investment	Ratio of Foregone Earnings to Gross Physical Investment
1920	.026	.016
1930	.076	.037
1940	.082	.040
1950	.103	.062
1956	.121	.071

Source: The numerators from T. W. Schultz "Capital Formation by Education," Journal of Political Economy, December 1960, Table 6; the denominators from Simon Kuznets, Capital in the American Economy: Its Formation and Financing, Princeton for NBER, 1961, Table R-4, p. 490.

[25] See *Educational Status, College Plans, and Occupational Status of Farm and Non-farm Youths: October 1959,* Tables D, and 12-16; also E. Roper, *Factors Affecting the Admission of High School Seniors to College,* Washington, 1949.

[26] See, for example, the estimates of "tastes for discrimination" in my *Economics of Discrimination,* Chapters 7-8.

[27] For example, Marshall alleged that much of the value of land in Great Britain resulted from the prestige attached to ownership (see his unpublished lecture, "Progress and Poverty," delivered March 6, 1883, and recently mimeographed by G. J. Stigler).

about 8 per cent in 1940 to 12 per cent in 1956. Foregone earnings, which are a rough measure of private investment, rose no less rapidly.[28] So the private real rate of return has apparently been higher on college education than on physical capital. Since the money rate has probably also been higher (see section 1), the evidence on real rates does not necessarily mean that the psychic rate has been higher on college education than on physical capital, but only that it could not have been much lower.

[28] Of course gross investment in education may have risen faster because the cost rather than the quantity of education rose faster. Unfortunately, no one has developed a good measure of the quantity of education; the most reasonable available measure is the number of persons receiving a college education. Since 1940 the number of college graduates in the labor force has much more than doubled while the real value of the capital stock has increased by less than 70 per cent (see my Table 15 and Denison, Table 12).

CHAPTER VI

Rates of Return from High-School Education and Trends over Time

THE first section of this chapter investigates the effect of high-school education on earnings and productivity, and the second changes over time in the economic effects of higher education. The first considers the effect of differential ability on the apparently large rate of return from high-school and thus on the apparently "decreasing returns" to additional years of schooling; the second considers whether the rapid secular increase in the number of high-school and college graduates in the United States has been accompanied by a secular decline in their rates of return.

1. The Rate of Return from High-School Education

Rates of return were computed for the 1939 cohort of urban, native-white, male high-school graduates and the 1949 cohort of all white male graduates using Census data and adjustments similar to those made for college graduates.[1] The best single private estimates, unadjusted for differential ability, average about 18 per cent, being 16 and 20 per cent for the 1939 and 1949 cohorts, respectively. These are several percentage points greater than the corresponding estimates for college graduates.

Table 12 suggests that the ability of high-school and elementary-school graduates differs considerably: the average I.Q. of high-school graduates is more than 30 per cent higher than that of persons with seven or eight years of schooling. A correction for differential ability might well have a larger effect on the estimated rate of return to high-school than to college graduates since the average I.Q. of the latter is

[1] See section 1 of Chapter IV and Appendix A.

TABLE 12

AVERAGE I.Q. AT SEVERAL EDUCATIONAL LEVELS

Educational Level	Average I.Q.
High-school graduates	112.0
High-school drop-outs	98.0
7-8 years of schooling	84.9

Source: Estimated from President's Commission on Higher Education, Higher Education for American Democracy, Washington, 1947, Volume VI, Table 11, p. 11; the data compiled by V. Benson give very similar results (see her "The Intelligence and Later Scholastic Success of Sixth Grade Pupils," School and Society, February 1942, p. 165, Table 1). Her data are especially interesting because the subsequent education of children given I.Q. tests in the sixth grade was determined. Therefore, the positive relation between I.Q. and education in her study cannot be considered a consequence of the education itself.

only about 12 per cent higher (see Table 4). Unfortunately, adjusted high-school rates cannot be estimated very easily. For example, the unadjusted rate of return to high-school drop-outs cannot be used because Table 12 indicates that their I.Q. is also much greater than that of elementary-school graduates; some confirmation is given by the fact that their unadjusted rate is only slightly below that to graduates.

Two estimates are available. Morgan and David have adjusted crude earnings differentials for father's education, personality, and several other variables.[2] The adjusted differential between high-school and elementary-school graduates is 64 per cent of the unadjusted differentials at ages 18-34 and 40 per cent at ages 35-74, while these ratios were 60 and 88 per cent between college and high-school graduates.[3] Thus their adjustments generally reduce the apparent gain from

[2] See the full description in section 2 of Chapter IV.

[3] In line with the above expectation, the crude differential between high-school drop-outs and elementary-school persons was not unaffected but was reduced by more than 60 per cent at ages 35-74 (computed from their Table III in "Education and Income," *Quarterly Journal of Economics,* August 1963; it was, however, increased slightly at the younger ages). One should point out, however, that the crude differentials between high-school graduates, drop-outs, and elementary-school graduates are probably significantly understated in their survey. For example, they find that the present values of the earnings of white male nonfarmer high-school graduates and drop-outs are about equal when only a 4 per cent interest rate is used, and drop-outs actually earn more than graduates at ages 18-35 (see *ibid.,* Table IV). Yet not only the Census data but also other quantitative evidence (see, e.g., *School and Early Employment Experience of Youth,* Dept. of Labor, Bulletin 1277, Washington, 1960, pp. 32-33) and general observations suggest that the relative earnings of graduates are much larger than that.

a high-school education by more than that from a college education.

A similar conclusion emerges from the study cited earlier of differentials between brothers.[4] Brothers averaging 11.8 years of schooling earned about $111 more (in 1939 prices) for each additional year of schooling than those averaging 8.9 years. This was about 73 per cent of the crude and 62 per cent of the corrected gains for high-school graduates of the same age in 1939.[5] Corresponding percentages for college graduates were 81 and 67.

The unadjusted rate of return to white male high-school graduates is greater than that to college graduates,[6] and the unadjusted rate to elementary-school graduates would be still greater. Such evidence

TABLE 13

INVESTMENT IN HIGH–SCHOOL EDUCATION, COLLEGE EDUCATION,
AND PHYSICAL CAPITAL, 1900–56
(current prices)

	Per Cent of 17-Year Olds with 12 Years of Schooling (1)	Rate of Total Investment in High School to Gross Physical Investment (2)	Ratio of Fore-gone Earnings in High School to Gross Physical Investment (3)	Ratio of Investment in High School to Investment in College (4)
1900	6.4	.021	.015	.900
1920	16.8	.041	.030	1.575
1930	29.0	.124	.071	1.625
1940	50.8	.146	.084	1.789
1950	59.0	.107	.066	1.033
1956	62.3	.133	.080	1.105

Source: Col. 1: <u>Historical Statistics of the United States, Colonial Times to 1957</u>, Washington, 1960, Series H223-233, p. 207; numerators in other columns from T.W. Schultz, "Capital Formation by Education," <u>Journal of Political Economy</u>, December 1960, Table 5; denominators from sources given in Table 11.

might well suggest "diminishing returns" or "diminishing marginal product" from additional years of schooling. Adjustments for differential ability, however, seem to reduce the apparent rate more to

[4] Donald E. Gorseline, *The Effects of Schooling Upon Income*, Bloomington, 1932. See section 2 of Chapter IV for a discussion of this study.

[5] The brothers with higher and lower educations averaged about 43 and 44 years old, respectively (*ibid.*). Earning differentials between them were compared to differentials in 1939 between persons aged 35-44 and 45-54, and a simple average taken.

[6] However, as indicated in the discussion in Chapter IV, section 3, the results are different for nonwhites: for example, the unadjusted rate of return to southern, male, nonwhite high-school graduates in 1939 is a few percentage points lower than that to college graduates.

high-school than to college graduates, and, I may add, probably still more to elementary-school graduates. So the appearance of diminishing returns results at least in part from the nature of the correlation between ability and education. Fully adjusted rates, therefore, might show no diminishing returns and might even show "increasing returns" to additional years of schooling.

The very rapid secular growth in high-school education in the United States (see Table 13) may in the first place be mostly due to compulsory school laws but is probably ultimately more directly related to anticipated private and social real rates of return. Evidence has already been presented indicating that the unadjusted private money rate of return to high-school education is very large, and although the adjusted rate may be much lower, it too is probably considerable. A first approximation to the unadjusted social money rate can be found by relating before-tax earning differentials to total costs: it is only slightly lower than the private rate for white males because differential tax payments almost offset public costs. The true social rate, moreover, would be much larger still if high-school education made an important contribution to the residual advance in knowledge (see the discussion in section 2 of Chapter V). So both the private and social rates of return seem sufficient to justify the large expansion of high-school education.

2. *Trends in Rates of Return*

Many issues of current importance depend on the secular trends in rates of return from education. For example, youngsters are now being exhorted to finish high school and even college partly because of a belief that relatively unskilled and uneducated persons are becoming increasingly obsolete in the American economy. This belief presumes that advances in technology have raised the gains from high-school and college education, especially since World War II, and perhaps even for a much longer period. On the other hand, economists have frequently alleged that the secular increase in the relative supply of more educated persons in the United States and elsewhere has reduced and will continue to reduce the gains from education.[7] In this section

---

[7] A forceful argument along these lines even in the context of the early postwar period can be found in S. Harris, *How Shall We Pay for Education?*, New York, 1948, pp. 61-72. For an earlier statement, see A. G. B. Fisher, "Education and Relative Wage Rates," *International Labour Review*, June 1932.

I try to provide some very preliminary answers to such questions by bringing together readily available evidence on secular trends.

AFTER 1939

Column 1 of Table 14 provides estimated private rates of return, unadjusted for differential ability, to college graduates in 1939, 1949, 1956, 1958, 1959, and 1961. The estimates for 1939 and 1949 were computed from data in the 1940 and 1950 Census and presented in

TABLE 14

PRIVATE RATES OF RETURN FROM COLLEGE AND HIGH-SCHOOL
EDUCATION FOR SELECTED YEARS SINCE 1939
(per cent)

Year of Cohort	College Graduates (1)	High-School Graduates (2)
1939	14.5	16
1949	13+	20
1956	12.4	25
1958	14.8	28
1959 1961	} slightly higher than in 1958	

Source: For 1939, 1949, 1956, and 1958, see Appendix A.
For 1959, see U.S. Summary Detailed Characteristics, U.S. Census
of Population, Table 223; for 1961, see Income of Families and
Persons in the United States, 1961, Current Population Reports,
p. 60, No. 39, Table 28.
   The 1959 estimates were based simply on a comparison of the
differences between the mean incomes of all males of 25 and over
in 1958 and 1959. Differentials between college and high-school
graduates were higher in 1959 by 7 per cent and between the latter
and elementary-school graduates by 11 per cent. Costs apparently
rose by a slightly smaller amount during the same period. The
1961 estimates were based on comparisons of median income differentials at various ages in 1958 and 1961. They were generally
higher in 1961, again by amounts probably slightly in excess of
the rise in costs during the same three years. More precise comparisons may change these estimates somewhat, probably not much.

Chapter IV. Although from a common source, they are not strictly comparable since the 1940 Census gave the earnings of urban, native-white males, whereas the 1950 Census gave the incomes of all white males. The estimates for 1956 and 1958 are based on the incomes of all males rather than whites alone as in 1949; more importantly, they were collected in surveys that often give considerably different results from those obtained in the Census. The entries for 1959 are rough estimates based simply on comparisons between mean income differentials computed from the 1960 Census and from the 1958 survey for all males over age 25. The entries for 1961 are based on similar comparisons between median differentials at different age classes. A fuller treatment of the 1960 Census materials and the 1961 survey is certainly warranted as more information on costs and incomes becomes available.

The rate of return apparently declined about 1.5 percentage points from 1939 to 1949 and then rose again in the late 1950's. Although these variations can hardly be considered statistically significant given the differences and errors in the basic data, the decline from 1939 to 1949 is consistent with extensive evidence of a general narrowing of skill differentials during the 1940's, and the rise from 1949 is consistent with the slight general widening during the 1950's. There apparently has been little net change in the private rate of return to male college graduates during the twenty-three years as a whole.

Private rates of return to high-school graduates for the same years are shown in column 2.[8] In contrast with the rates for college graduates, these rose throughout the period, by 4 points from 1939 to 1949, and by a whopping 8 points after 1949, so there was about a 12-point increase during the twenty-three years as a whole. Apparently, the economic position of high-school graduates remained about the same relative to college graduates and increased substantially relative to elementary-school graduates. Note, however, that since the rates in Table 14 are unadjusted for differential ability, the true rates would have moved differently since 1939 if the correlation between ability and education changed. One might well believe that the differential ability of high-school graduates rose over time because now only the physically handicapped, dullards, or least-motivated persons fail to go to high school. Although this might explain the large rise in the unadjusted gain from high school, note that Morgan and David actually find a larger ratio of adjusted to unadjusted earnings differentials between high-school and elementary-school graduates at younger than at older ages. The ratios between college and high-school graduates, on the other hand, are smaller at younger ages.[9]

The movements in rates since 1939 were the net result of several changes with different effects. The substantial advance in technology and knowledge would tend to increase rates of return on education,

[8] Since nonwhites are concentrated at lower educational levels, the last four estimates would be biased more when comparing rates of return from high-school than from college. Comparisons made with the 1950 Census data indicate, however, that only a small upward bias could have resulted from including nonwhites.

[9] Computed from *Quarterly Journal of Economics*, August 1963, Table III.

even if the advance was "neutral" and did not change percentage differentials (see my argument in Chapter III, section 2), and even if the advance was itself an effect of education. Demand for well-educated persons has also risen since 1939 because of a shift in government and business toward complicated military hardware and systematic research.

On the other hand, a growth in the relative number of highly educated persons would, by itself, reduce rates of return on education. Table 15 indicates that the number of college and high-school graduates has increased at about the same rate since 1939, so there is apparently little reason from the supply side to expect much decline in percentage earning differentials between them. Yet these changes in supply would produce a decline in the rate of return from college education. For the earnings of college and high-school graduates

TABLE 15

PERCENTAGE OF POPULATION WITH HIGH-SCHOOL AND
COLLEGE EDUCATION IN 1940, 1950, AND 1957

Year	High-School Graduates	College Graduates
1940	12	5
1950	18	7
1957	22	9

Source: H. Miller, "Annual and Lifetime Income in Relation to Education, 1939-1959," *American Economic Review*, December 1960, Table 2.

would decline relative to less-educated persons, and thus absolute earning differentials between college and high-school graduates would decline even if percentage differentials were unchanged. And a decline in absolute differentials would lower the rate of return from college unless costs declined by an equal amount. Once again a change in percentage differentials gives a wrong picture even of the direction of change in rates of return.

A decrease in mortality would by itself—the earnings of survivors taken as given—increase rates of return (see Chapter III, section 2). Mortality among white adults was already so low in 1939, however, that subsequent decreases could only increase rates by a minor amount. To illustrate, suppose that no member of the 1939 cohorts ever died, and that earnings beyond age 64 rose at a rate of 2 per cent per year. The rate of return to white males in 1939 would have been less than one half of a percentage point above the rate computed with 1940 mortality conditions.

If adjusted rates behaved similarly to unadjusted ones, the rate of return from college did not change on balance and that from high school increased substantially after 1939. Therefore, advances in technology and other forces increasing the demand for educated persons must have offset the increase in college graduates and more than offset the increase in high-school graduates. Consequently, technological advance and other changes apparently increased the demand for high-school graduates more than that for college graduates.

BEFORE 1939

The growth in technology, shifts in demand, decline in mortality, growth in education, etc., clearly may not have occurred at the same rate in the early part of the century as they did subsequently. About technology and demand shifts, little can be said.[10] Mortality, however, definitely declined more rapidly in the early part of the century. For example, if the mortality of white males in 1901 had prevailed in 1939, rates of return to college and high-school education would have been about three-fifths of a percentage point lower than they were with 1939 mortality.

Although the relative number of both high-school and college graduates increased substantially before 1939, the former probably increased more rapidly. Supply changes alone, therefore, would produce a greater decline in the rate of return to high-school than to college graduates. Indeed, they would have *increased* the rate to college graduates if a widening percentage differential between college and high-school earnings more than offset a decline in the earnings of both relative to less-educated persons.[11]

Quantitative information before 1939 is extremely scanty and unreliable, and Tables 16 and 17 summarize the little information available. Table 16 presents absolute income differentials in both current and 1958 dollars between college and high-school graduates at scattered dates, while Table 17 presents similar differentials between

10 Denison's calculations suggest greater technological progress since the late 1920's only if Department of Commerce rather than Kendrick-Kuznets estimates of national product are used (see his *Sources of Economic Growth in the United States,* New York, 1962, p. 269).

11 Note that once again a widening percentage differential may be consistent with a declining rate of return even if costs were unchanged.

TABLE 16

INCOME DIFFERENTIALS BETWEEN COLLEGE AND HIGH-SCHOOL GRADUATES AT
VARIOUS AGES AND FOR SCATTERED YEARS SINCE 1904 IN
CURRENT AND 1958 DOLLARS

	1904 Mean Earnings		1926 Median Incomes		1927 Mean Incomes		1956-58 (current dollars)	
Age	Current Dollars (1)	1958 Dollars (2)	Current Dollars (3)	1958 Dollars (4)	Current Dollars (5)	1958 Dollars (6)	Mean Incomes (7)	Median Incomes (8)
25-34			1,146	1,870	834	1,361	1,915	1,127
32	936	3,019						
30-34			1,465	2,390			1,438	
35-44			2,821	4,602			4,068	2,478

Source

Col. 1: J. M. Dodge, "The Money Value of Technical Training," <u>Transactions of the American Society of Mechanical Engineers</u>, vol. 25, 1904.
Col. 3: Lord, <u>Relation of Education and Income</u>.
Col. 5: Gorseline, <u>Effect of Schooling</u>.
Col. 7: Miller in <u>American Economic Review</u>, December 1960, Table 1, p. 965.

high-school and elementary-school graduates. According to the 1926 survey,[12] real absolute differentials between college and high-school graduates declined substantially from the 1920's to the 1950's. Since real costs rose during this period, rates of return to college would have declined even more.[13] According to the same survey, however, real differentials between high-school and elementary-school graduates[14] widened greatly during the same period. These data do not necessarily imply, therefore, that rates of return to high-school graduates declined during the last thirty years.

While rates of return from college education may have greatly declined at the same time that rates from high school declined much less, if at all, the accuracy and comparability with later data of the 1926 survey are subject to doubt. For one thing, questionnaires were sent out through a single fraternity, and the response rate was low (about 50 per cent). Only 1,750 persons in the final sample were college graduates, and many were business majors. Moreover, the differentials between high-school and elementary-school graduates seem

[12] Everett W. Lord, *The Relation of Education to Income*, Indianapolis, 1928.

[13] These data constitute Renshaw's principal evidence of secular decline in rates of return from college education (see "Estimating the Returns to Education," *Review of Economics and Statistics*, August 1960, p. 322).

[14] The survey clearly overstates these differentials because all persons with at least eight years of schooling are lumped together in the category I call "elementary-school graduates."

TABLE 17

INCOME DIFFERENTIALS BETWEEN HIGH-SCHOOL AND ELEMENTARY-SCHOOL GRADUATES AT VARIOUS AGES AND FOR SCATTERED YEARS SINCE 1900 IN CURRENT AND 1958 DOLLARS

Age	1900-06 Mean Earnings		1908 Mean Earnings		1927 Mean Incomes		1956-58 Mean Incomes, 1958 Dollars	1926 Median Incomes		1956-58 Median Incomes, 1958 Dollars
	Current Dollars (1)	1958 Dollars (2)	Current Dollars (3)	1958 Dollars (4)	Current Dollars (5)	1958 Dollars (6)	(7)	Current Dollars (8)	1958 Dollars (9)	(10)
20	300	980	275	862						
21	425	1,389		1,332						
22	500	1,634	425							
23	500	1,634								
24	625	2,042	500	1,724						
25	900	2,941	862	2,702						
25-34	494	1,614					1,222	316	515	1,616
35-44	722	2,359			} 403	658	1,724	866	1,413	1,785
45-54										

Source

Cols. 1, 3: A.C. Ellis, The Money Value of Education, U.S. Office of Education Bulletin 22, Washington, 1917.
Col. 5: Gorseline, Effects of Schooling, Table XXXIV, p. 113.
Cols. 7, 10: Miller in American Economic Review, December 1960, Table 1, p. 965.
Col. 8: Lord, Relation of Education and Income, p. 8.

133

unbelievably small compared to those between college and high-school graduates.

Several persons around the turn of the century studied the effect of education on incomes in a few cities, companies, specialties, or schools. They found much larger differentials between college, high-school, and elementary-school graduates than are found today (see Tables 16 and 17). Since the real costs of schooling rose rapidly over time,[15] this evidence suggests a large decline in rates of return to both high-school and college education.

If the data before 1940 can be considered representative, which is questionable, rates of return on both high-school and college education declined rather significantly during the first forty years of the century, and then stopped declining and even rose during the next twenty years. Since at least the relative number of college graduates increased more rapidly after 1940 and since mortality declined more rapidly before, these very different trends would probably be explained by less rapid shifts in the demand for educated persons during the earlier period: advances in knowledge and shifts in demand for final products may have been less favorable to educated persons then.[16] This conclusion is sufficiently important that much more attention should be paid to the historical evidence.[17]

One can also learn much from comparisons of different countries. A particularly good example of an "autonomous" increase in the supply of higher education is provided by the influx of well-educated European Jews into Palestine during the twenties and thirties, an influx motivated by religious and cultural considerations, not by any economic demand for well-educated persons. The influx should have lowered the return to higher education, and recent evidence indicates private rates of return in Israel during the fifties of only about 6 and 9 per cent for high-school graduates and college persons respectively.[18] An equally

[15] Total costs per student in 1947-49 dollars were as follows in 1900 and 1950:

	High School	College
1900	320	1,050
1950	1,035	2,415

See Schultz in *Journal of Political Economy*, December 1960, Tables 5-7. His figures were converted from current to 1947-49 dollars with the Consumer Price Index.

[16] Historians usually do assume that the technological improvements accompanying the industrial revolution reduced the relative demand for highly skilled persons.

[17] Albert Fishlow has, in fact, started to study (for the National Bureau) the historical trends in the demand for and supply of educated persons in the United States.

[18] See R. Klinov-Malul, "The Profitability of Investment in Education in Israel," unpublished Ph.D. dissertation, Hebrew University, 1964, Chapter 3.

autonomous change has been the large-scale immigration of low-educated African and Asian Jews to Israel after its birth in 1948. This change should have increased the return to higher education, and, notwithstanding the equalitarian tradition in Israel, there is clear evidence of a significant increase after 1948.[19]

19 See *ibid.*, Chapter 4; also V. Bahral, *The Effect of Mass Immigration on Wages in Israel* (mimeographed) , Falk Project for Economic Research in Israel, 1962.

CHAPTER VII

Age, Earnings, Wealth, and Human Capital

VIRTUALLY all the implications of the theory of investment in human capital developed in Part One depend directly or indirectly on the effect of human capital on the earnings and productivity of persons and firms. Consequently most of my empirical work has been concentrated on measuring and assessing these effects. Chapters IV through VI contain the results for various demographic groups and time periods in the United States.

Several investigators have examined a variety of other implications, and the additional empirical support given to the theory has been quite gratifying.[1] Thus Oi independently developed an analysis of the effect of investment in human capital on unemployment and turnover that is quite similar to ours, and tested it empirically in a number of ways.[2] Smith applied the analysis to the turnover of skilled personnel in the military, and developed rules for increasing the efficiency of their expenditures on personnel.[3] Mincer applied the analysis in estimating the amounts spent on on-the-job training, and then used his estimates to understand the income and employment behavior of

---

[1] Recently a criticism was made of this theory largely on the grounds of lack of realism and relevance (see R. S. Eckaus, "Investment in Human Capital: A Comment," *Journal of Political Economy*, October 1963). Instead of quarreling with details of his comment—and there are several that seem wrong or misleading—I would like to urge that the evidence provided by this chapter and the previous ones, by the studies mentioned here, and by several other studies not yet completed indicates that the theory is quite useful in interpreting the real world.

[2] See Walter Y. Oi "Labor as a Quasi-fixed Factor of Production," unpublished Ph.D. dissertation, University of Chicago, 1961, and "Labor as a Quasi-fixed Factor," *Journal of Political Economy*, December 1962.

[3] See G. Smith "Differential Pay for Military Technicians," unpublished Ph.D. dissertation, Columbia University, 1964.

different groups.[4] In an earlier and pioneering article, Mincer had already developed and tested a theory that related the distribution of earnings to the distribution of investments in human capital.[5] Or to take a final and very different example, Clara Friedman has neatly used the human capital approach to show that virtually nobody enters the New York City public school teaching system with more than the minimum required schooling because the value of the additional pay given for additional schooling is less than the cost of postponed earnings.[6]

This chapter covers still another aspect: the effect of human capital on earnings and wealth at different ages. The first part deals with the steepness and shape of the well-known age-earnings profiles. Since these are relevant in studying the declining incomes of older persons or the low incomes of younger persons, the effect of learning on productivity, and many other life-cycle changes, a demonstration that their shape is determined by investment in human capital should be of considerable interest.

In recent years there has been a noticeable shift of emphasis in economic theorizing and data collection from income and flows to capital and stocks. This surely is the thrust of the permanent income and related hypotheses in consumption studies,[7] of the emphasis on the allocation of assets in monetary theory,[8] and of the attention paid to the capital aspects of expenditures on durable goods.[9] In line with this shift, life-cycle economic changes should be related not only or even primarily to changes in earnings and other income, but also to changes in human and other wealth. Accordingly, the second part of this chapter develops the concept of age-wealth profiles—the relation between age and the discounted value of subsequent earnings—and

[4] See J. Mincer, "On-the-Job Training: Costs, Returns, and Some Implications," *Investment in Human Beings*, NBER Special Conference 15, supplement to *Journal of Political Economy*, October 1962, pp. 50-59.

[5] See his "Investment in Human Capital and Personal Income Distribution," *Journal of Political Economy*, August 1958.

[6] See her "Differential Pay of New York City School Teachers," unpublished Ph.D. dissertation, Columbia University, 1962.

[7] See M. Friedman, *A Theory of the Consumption Function*, Princeton for NBER, 1957; and F. Modigliani and R. Brumberg, "Utility Analysis and the Consumption Function: An Interpretation of Cross-Section Data" in *Post-Keynesian Economics*, ed. by K. K. Kurihara, New Brunswick, 1954.

[8] See J. Tobin, "Money, Capital and Other Stores of Value," *American Economic Review*, May 1961; or M. Friedman "The Quantity Theory of Money—A Restatement" in M. Friedman, ed., *Studies in the Quantity Theory of Money*, Chicago, 1956.

[9] See R. W. Goldsmith, *A Study of Saving in the United States*, Princeton, 1955-56.

shows that their shape, like that of the underlying age-earnings profile, is determined by investment in human capital. A few applications illustrating the usefulness of age-wealth profiles and thus indirectly the importance of human capital conclude the discussion.

1. Age-Earnings Profiles

Table 18 shows the mean net after-tax incomes in 1939 and 1949 of males classified by age and years of schooling; the word "net" indi-

TABLE 18

NET AFTER-TAX INCOMES OF WHITE MALES IN 1939
AND 1949, BY AGE AND YEARS OF EDUCATION
(dollars)

Age	16+ (1)	12 (2)	7 and 8[a] (3)
		1939	
14–21	29	360	457
22–24	1,185	1,136	925
25–29	1,930	1,494	1,182
30–34	2,839	1,929	1,453
35–44	3,878	2,488	1,768
45–54	4,361	2,744	1,935
55–64	3,856	2,527	1,773
		1949	
14–21	42	705	795
22–24	1,794	2,151	1,769
25–29	2,929	2,763	2,185
30–34	4,380	3,218	2,498
35–44	6,295	3,623	2,778
45–54	7,883	4,215	2,959
55–64	7,329	4,165	2,711

Source: See Tables 1 and 2 and Appendix A, section 1.

[a]For 1939, 7 and 8 years of schooling; for 1949, 8 years.

cates that direct outlays on schooling have been subtracted from reported incomes. Although the analysis in this chapter does not at all depend on the use of such an income concept, I have done so because foregone income—an important part of the total cost of education—is implicitly subtracted from reported incomes. Economic analysis as well as consistent accounting would be made easier either if direct outlays were also subtracted or if foregone income was added back. Since the discussion in Chapter II indicates that *all* the costs of general on-the-job training and of certain other investments are implicitly subtracted from reported incomes, comparability among different kinds of human capital is most easily achieved by explicitly subtracting direct school outlays, which brings us to the net income concept used in Table 18.

The table clearly shows that average incomes at each age class are strongly related to education, a relation explored in the previous chapters. The table also shows that incomes tend to be relatively low at the beginning of labor force participation, rise throughout later ages until a common peak is reached in the 45-54 age class, and decline in the last age class. Although the peaks are reached in the same *class*, they are not necessarily reached at the same *age*. For example, if incomes continually increased to the peak age and continually declined thereafter, actual peak ages could be anywhere from 35 to 64, a spread of 30 years, and yet all the observed peaks might occur in the 45-54 age class.

Therefore, these data do not necessarily contradict the common notion that unskilled persons reach their peak earnings before skilled persons. This notion has been based, however, on misleading statistics. Since occupation changes with age, the more able tending to rise and the less able to fall in the occupational hierarchy, earnings in different occupations at a given moment in time might show an earlier peak in unskilled occupations merely because older unskilled workers are less able than younger ones. Education statistics are less affected because education is usually completed at an early age.

Table 18 gives the incomes of different cohorts at a moment in time, not those of a given cohort aging over time. Age-income profiles based on longitudinal or time series data can differ from those based on cross-sectional data because of business cycles, secular trends toward higher education, and occupation or life-cycle employment changes (see the discussion in the beginning of Chapter IV). Probably the most important, pervasive, and calculable difference results, however, from the secular growth in incomes, which implies, for example, that the cohort of college graduates aged 25 in 1939 received a higher real income at age 35 than did the cohort aged 35 in 1939. Since secular growth in the United States has been large, averaging almost 2 per cent per person per annum, the difference would be considerable.

The cross-sectional education profiles have been converted into time series profiles only by adjusting very simply for the secular growth in incomes. The income t years later of a cohort finishing its schooling in a base year was estimated by multiplying the base year income of

CHART 2

"Time Series" Age-Earnings Profiles for Several 1939 Education Cohorts

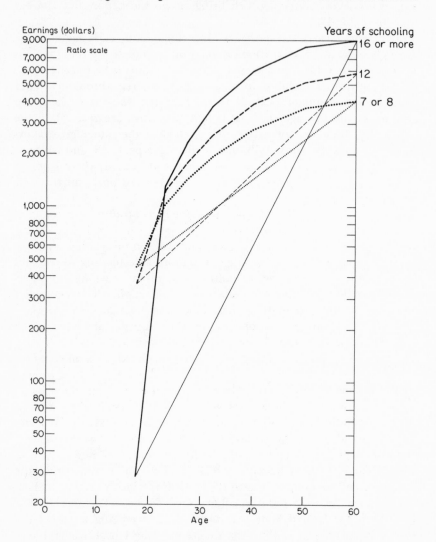

the cohort with the same schooling and t years older by $(1.02)^t$, where 2 per cent is the assumed average annual growth in incomes. For example, the cohort of college graduates aged 35-44 in 1939 had an income of $3,400, and the estimated income at age 35 of a cohort graduating from college in 1939 at age 22 would be $3,400 multiplied by $(1.02)^{13}$. Chart 2 plots such time series profiles for college, high-school, and elementary-school graduates of 1939.

This adjustment for secular growth is inaccurate on several counts. Although 2 per cent is a good estimate of the average growth in real per capita income since the 1880's, the growth during the last twenty-five years, especially in after-tax incomes, has been less. Moreover, Chapter VI suggests that incomes of less-educated persons grew more rapidly before 1940 and possibly less rapidly after 1940 than those of more educated persons. Consequently, a more accurate adjustment of recent data would have a lower average rate of growth and different rates at different educational levels. Since, however, none of the conclusions reached in this chapter would be greatly affected, I have retained a simple 2 per cent adjustment. The rate of return estimates in Chapters IV through VI are more sensitive, and different adjustments were tried there.

The profiles in Chart 2 do not decline at older ages, but continue to rise through age 65, the last age covered by the data. This perhaps surprising conclusion can be checked with data from surveys taken at

TABLE 19

ESTIMATED INCOMES OVER TIME OF COHORTS AT DIFFERENT
EDUCATIONAL LEVELS
(dollars)

Age of Cohort in 1939	Income of Cohort in		
	1939	1949	1958
	COLLEGE GRADUATES		
25-34	5,155	8,960	12,269
35-44	8,386	11,543	10,966
45-54	9,430	10,732	--
55-64	8,338	--	--
	HIGH-SCHOOL GRADUATES		
25-34	3,699	4,812	6,295
35-44	5,380	5,770	6,510
45-54	5,933	5,798	--
55-64	5,464	--	--
	ELEMENTARY-SCHOOL GRADUATES		
25-34	2,848	3,610	4,337
35-44	3,823	3,896	3,960
45-54	4,182	3,586	--
55-64	3,833	--	--

Source: Tables 1 and 2 and Appendix A, section 1.

different times, which provide an independent measure of the change over time in a cohort's income. For example, college graduates aged 45-54 in 1939 would be 55-64 years old in 1949, and the real incomes of 45- to 54-year-old college graduates in the 1940 Census could be compared with those of 55- to 64-year-old college graduates in the 1950 Census. Such evidence is not altogether reliable since the income concept is not the same in different surveys, sampling and response errors abound, and so on; nevertheless, it can serve as a check. Table 19, which brings together data from the 1940 and 1950 Census, and from a Census survey in 1958, indicates that a cohort's income increases more with age than is shown by cross-section data. In particular, there is no systematic tendency for time series profiles to decline in the last age class even though cross-section ones do.[10] The decline in the latter has been responsible for an erroneous inference about the shape of the former[11] which has made for misunderstanding of the economic position of older workers. For example, their retirement at 65 has been misinterpreted because their earnings have been assumed to be way below their peak earnings rather than possibly higher than ever.

The time series and cross-section profiles would be identical in a stationary economy since they differ only because of the growth in per capita earnings. If growth were due to the operation of forces, like neutral technological changes, that uniformly raised earnings at all ages, cross-sectional profiles would be unaffected, while time series profiles would decline to the former if growth ceased. If, on the other hand, growth were due to the embodiment of new technology in younger (i.e., "newer") workers, or to other improvements in the economic effects of the human capital invested in successive cohorts with the same number of school years, cross-sectional profiles would

[10] The result may be due to selective retirement before the age of 65, since persons whose earnings would decline most might elect to retire early. I owe this point to J. Mincer.

[11] Whether Marshall's statement that occupation profiles eventually turn down held for time series profiles in nineteenth century England is not clear. Many related statements for the United States, however, make no allowance for growth and thus incorrectly jump from cross-section data to a longitudinal inference. To take one of many possible examples, H. Miller said, " . . . When he [the average male worker] is in his forties or early fifties he has usually attained the peak of his earning power, and from that time until he is ready to retire from the labor market his annual earnings shrink until they are not any higher than those he received as a young man." (*Income of the American People,* New York, 1955, p. 64.) He then refers to cross-section data that would not decline (at least up to the age of 65) if adjusted for the annual growth in earnings.

be affected by growth and would approach the shape of the time series profiles if growth ceased. For example, if new technology were embodied in younger workers, they would have greater technological knowledge than older workers, so cross-sectional profiles would understate, while time series profiles would accurately measure, the effect of age on the earnings of workers with the same technological knowledge. So even though the time series profiles were derived from cross-sectional ones by adjusting for growth, they may more accurately describe the relation between age and earnings in a stationary economy. In particular, earnings may not decline before age 65 even in such an economy.

Although all the profiles in Chart 2 rise continuously, they do so at very different rates, the average rate of increase being positively related to education. This is apparent from the lines connecting incomes at ages 14-21 with those at 55-64, for they have slopes of 15, 7, and 5.5 per cent, respectively, for college, high-school, and elementary-school graduates. The analysis in Part One indicated that investment in human capital steepens age-earnings profiles because earnings are net of investment costs at younger ages and gross of returns at older ages. Indeed, the proposition could be turned around and if two profiles differed in steepness, the steeper could be said to indicate the presence of greater human capital. Consequently, the positive relation between steepness and education in Chart 2 seems to support this approach.

It does, but note that the data plotted there include the effects of all investments in human capital, including vocational and on-the-job training, health, knowledge of economic opportunities, etc., as well as education. College graduates could have more education than high-school graduates and less total capital because, for example, the latter had more on-the-job and vocational training. If so, high-school graduates would have lower net earnings at younger ages, higher earnings later on, and a steeper profile than college graduates. Since the contrary is indicated, the main inference must be that there is a positive correlation between education and total capital.[12] This inference is

---

[12] The net earnings of young persons in Chart 2 are overestimated because the direct costs of certain investments (such as migration and health) do not tend to be subtracted from earnings. The overestimate is probably not too large, however, because many direct costs (such as on-the-job training and education) are subtracted, and indirect costs are usually more important than direct costs. Moreover, earnings at older ages would include the return on all investments, and they are clearly directly related to education.

quite sensible because education is presumably an important part of the total, and other kinds of investment in human capital, such as health, migration, adult education, and on-the-job training, appear to be positively related to education (see Chapter IV, section 2).

The entries in Table 20 bring out precisely what should be apparent from even a cursory glance at Chart 2; namely, the profiles are quite concave to the age axis, especially at younger ages and higher educational levels. The concavity is shown by the continual decline in

TABLE 20

ANNUAL RATES OF INCOME CHANGE BETWEEN SUCCESSIVE AGE CLASSES
FOR 1939 COHORTS AT DIFFERENT EDUCATIONAL LEVELS

Education (years)	$t=23$ $t'=18$ (1)	$t=27$ $t'=23$ (2)	$t=32$ $t'=27$ (3)	$t=40$ $t'=32$ (4)	$t=50$ $t'=40$ (5)	$t=60$ $t'=50$ (6)	$t=60$ $t'=18$ (7)
16+	.43	.19	.10	.06	.03	.01	.05
12	.17	.09	.07	.05	.03	.01	.04
8	.14	.08	.06	.04	.03	.01	.04
Simple average	.25	.12	.08	.05	.03	.01	.04

Source: The data plotted in Chart 2. The entries are computed from the formula $\dfrac{Y_t - Y_{t'}}{Y_t + Y_{t'}} \times \dfrac{2}{t - t'}$, where Y_t is income at age t, and $Y_{t'}$ is income at age t'.

annual rates of increase between successive age classes, the declines being strongest at younger ages and higher educational levels. In addition, rates of increase of earnings with age differ appreciably only at younger ages; for example, the rate of increase is 30 percentage points higher for college than for elementary-school graduates between ages 18 and 23, while they increase at about the same rate between 40 and 60.

The theory developed in Part One also explains these results remarkably well. Earnings are depressed "artificially" during the investment period because costs are written off then, and rise unusually rapidly afterward because the depressant is released. A concave age-earnings profile results, especially near the investment period which is concentrated at younger ages. Since the total amount invested is positively correlated with education, more educated cohorts would have more concave profiles, again especially at younger ages. So a simple theory of investment in human capital can explain the differences in concavity as well as in steepness.

2. *Age-Wealth Profiles*

As pointed out in the introduction, in recent years there has been a shift in both theoretical and empirical work from flows to stocks, which suggests that, in studying life-cycle behavior, attention should be paid to age-wealth profiles as well as to the more familiar age-earnings profiles. This section discusses the influence of investment in human capital on the shape of age and human-wealth profiles (little direct attention is paid to nonhuman wealth).

Although the market value of human wealth cannot be determined directly because, happily, there no longer is a market in human beings, an indirect estimate can be based on the rule that the value of an asset equals the discounted sum of the income stream yielded. In other words, the value of the human wealth "owned" at a particular age would equal the discounted sum of subsequent earnings. So the shape of the relation between age and the discounted sum of subsequent earnings, which is called an age-wealth profile, would be completely determined by interest rates and the shape of age-earnings profiles.

If interest rates were zero, age-wealth profiles would decline continuously because wealth would simply be the sum of subsequent earnings and, consequently, would have to decline with age regardless of the shape of age-earnings profiles.[13] If interest rates were infinitely large, wealth and earnings profiles would be identical; in particular, the former would rise as long as the latter did. With interest rates between these extremes, wealth profiles would peak somewhere between the initial and the peak earnings age, closer to the latter the higher the rates.[14]

Although time series profiles are clearly more relevant in calculating cohort wealth profiles than cross-sectional ones are, even the former have to be modified because they consider only the earnings of cohort members alive and participating in the labor force. They could be converted into the relevant cohort profiles with an adjustment for the fraction not participating at different ages. Since participation declines with age, the differences between time series and cohort profiles would be greater at older ages, especially at lower

13 More precisely, they would rise only during periods of negative earnings. Since net earnings could be negative only during the investment period, even these rises would be at younger ages.

14 See section 2 of Appendix B.

educational levels; in particular, the latter profiles would tend to turn down before age 65 even though the former did not. The peak in cohort earnings would be later, however, than that in cross-sectional earnings.

If a cohort earnings profile did not rise much, the wealth profile would necessarily decline continuously, at least if interest rates did

CHART 3

Age-Wealth Profiles of 1939 Graduates

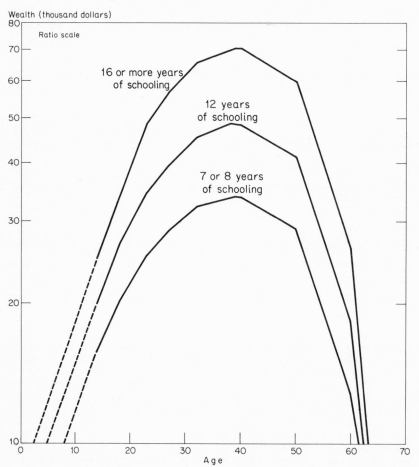

Note: Earnings discounted at an 8 per cent rate.

not decline much with age. If earnings rose sufficiently, wealth would also rise, and the rate of increase in wealth would be positively related to, yet less than, that in earnings. Although wealth necessarily peaks before earnings, the peak wealth age would be later, the greater the increase and the later the peak in earnings.[15] Since the increase in earnings is related to investment in human capital, the increase in wealth and its peak age would also be related to this investment.

Chart 3 illustrates these effects by graphing the wealth profiles of the 1939 cohorts of college, high-school, and elementary-school male graduates.[16] All earnings have been discounted at an 8 per cent interest rate, about the average rate of return on business capital (see section 1 of Chapter V). Time series earnings were only adjusted for mortality, still by far the major cause of nonparticipation before age 65.

All the wealth profiles rise for about the first twenty years of labor force participation and then decline. The rates of increase are positively related to education, although the differences here are smaller than those in earnings. Wealth peaks at about age 39, some fifteen years before cohort earnings do. The peaks in wealth are not much affected by education because neither the peaks in earnings nor their rates of increase after the early thirties are much affected by education (see Table 20).

Investment in human capital explains not only these differences in wealth profiles, but also changes over time. For example, in the early nineteenth century wealth profiles usually peaked quite early, say at age 20 or so,[17] because mortality was high and workers were usually relatively unskilled. Unskilled workers with high mortality rates

15 For proofs of these assertions, see sections 2-4 of Appendix B.

16 Chart 3 was computed from earnings figures that are slightly different from and presumably less accurate than those used in section 1. Since the more correct figures would yield very similar wealth profiles, I have not bothered to make any corrections.

17 The value of a typical male Negro slave rose until he was in his early twenties, reached a peak there, and then declined for the rest of his life. (See R. Evans, Jr., "The Economics of American Negro Slavery, 1830-1860," *Aspects of Labor Economics,* Special Conference 14, Princeton, for NBER, 1962, Table 12.) Since the value of slaves was determined by maintenance costs as well as productivity, the peak in the present value of subsequent productivity would have come still earlier, unless, as is unlikely, maintenance costs rose significantly during the late teens and early twenties. The present value of the earnings of unskilled free persons probably peaked at a similar age.

would have a flat or even declining (cohort) earnings profile,[18] and thus a continually declining wealth profile. The heavy investment in education, training, and health during the past hundred years has steepened the typical earnings profile and, consequently, shifted the typical peak wealth age to about 40.[19]

Before concluding, it might be wise to consider explicitly some applications of wealth profiles since they are less well known than earnings profiles and their importance may not be obvious to many readers. Two applications were chosen for their interest and timeliness. The first deals with the need to provide depreciation on human as well as physical capital and the second with life-cycle variations in savings.[20]

Many persons have suggested that a term accounting for the depreciation of human beings be subtracted from reported earnings. Irving Fisher, in his brilliant presentation of the conceptual foundations of the income and wealth concepts, said: "If it were true that income could never trench on capital, we could not reckon a laboring man's wages as income without first deducting a premium or sinking fund sufficient to provide for the continuance of this income after the destruction by death of the laborer."[21] If by "laboring man" is meant relatively unskilled, as seems reasonable, then Fisher's conclusion is supported by my analysis of age-wealth profiles. Since their earnings profile would not rise much with age, their wealth profile would tend to decline continuously. Wealth could be maintained constant, therefore, only if the rate of decline in wealth was subtracted from earnings at the same age and added to a depreciation or sinking fund.

In recent years emphasis has shifted from the laboring man to the educated man and from conceptual issues to more practical ones.

[18] There is some evidence that the productivity of male Negro slaves did not change much between their twenties and fifties (see J. R. Meyer and A. H. Conrad, "The Economics of Slavery in the Ante Bellum South," *Journal of Political Economy*, April 1958, p. 106).

[19] For example, the profiles plotted in Chart 3 would have peaked several years earlier if mortality rates of the middle-nineteenth century had been used.

[20] I omit possibly the most well-known application, namely, to the relation between age and life insurance. This stimulated the pioneering book by L. Dublin and A. Lotka, *The Money Value of a Man*, New York, 1930, revised in 1940. Also see B. Weisbrod, "The Valuation of Human Capital," *Journal of Political Economy*, October 1961, pp. 425-436. A related application is to damage suits resulting from disability or death. An absorbing example is given in the recent best seller by L. Nizer, *My Life in Court*, New York, 1961, Chapter 5, section II, entitled "The Worth of a Man."

[21] *Nature of Capital and Income*, New York, 1930, p. 111. Fisher, however, argued against the use of this "ideal" definition of income.

Tax laws are said to discriminate against education and other kinds of human capital because depreciation can be deducted only from the taxable income of physical capital.[22] Unquestionably, a more symmetrical tax treatment of these two classes of capital would be desirable. However, one should be aware that a good deal of depreciation on human capital occurs unknowingly. Thus, as pointed out elsewhere, part of the costs of human capital are "written off" immediately because foregone earnings are, in effect, deducted from accrued taxable income.[23] Since these indirect costs are about 75 per cent of the private costs of college education in the United States,[24] and an even higher percentage of general on-the-job training costs, the depreciation unknowingly permitted is considerable. Indeed, the present value of the amount so permitted would often be greater than that explicitly allowed on physical assets depreciated over a five- or ten-year or even longer period!

Some important relations between depreciation and human capital can be obtained using age-wealth profiles if true income were simply defined as the amount necessary to keep wealth intact.[25] Then the depreciation or "appreciation" necessary to convert reported into true earnings would simply equal the rate of change in wealth. Consequently, the depreciation could be said to be insufficient whenever wealth declined and excessive whenever it increased.

Since the wealth profile of unskilled workers would decline continuously, an explicit depreciation deduction is needed at each working age. The profiles of skilled workers, on the other hand, rise for a spell and the rises are larger and steeper, the greater the investment in human capital. Consequently, since their true earnings would actually be greater than reported earnings at younger ages and less only after the peak wealth age, an appreciation term would be required at all ages before the peak in wealth. So while tax laws can be said to discriminate against all unskilled and older skilled workers, they discriminate in *favor* of younger skilled workers. Of course, during the whole period of labor force participation there would be a net decline even in the wealth of skilled workers. But it would be

22 See T. W. Schultz, "Investment in Human Capital," *American Economic Review*, March 1961, p. 13, and R. Goode, "Educational Expenditures and the Income Tax," in S. J. Mushkin, ed., *Economics of Higher Education*, Washington, 1962. *

23 See Chapter II, section 1, and Chapter V, section 1.

24 See Chapter IV, section 1.

25 Such an ideal definition is not necessary for our purposes, but it does simplify the discussion.

relatively small: for example, using an 8 per cent interest rate, the average annual depreciation in the wealth of workers with a flat earnings profile (during an assumed forty-two-year earning period) would equal 30 per cent of average earnings while that of the 1939 cohort of college graduates would equal only 18 per cent of their earnings.[26]

So death rather than investment in human capital appears to be the main reason why reported earnings, on the whole, overestimate true earnings. When the former is the principal determinant of wealth changes, as with unskilled workers, depreciation bulks large relative to earnings, but when the latter is more important, as with skilled workers, depreciation becomes less important. Probably the major explanation of this paradoxical conclusion is that much depreciation is unknowingly permitted on human capital.

In recent years studies of household behavior have been greatly influenced by the argument that current expenditures depend not only on current income but also on expected future income.[27] In particular, total consumption at any age would be affected by expectations about incomes at later ages. So life-cycle variations in consumption would not match those in earnings because the latter would be at least partly anticipated and then offset by appropriate savings and dissavings.[28] It shall be demonstrated that this new approach makes life-cycle changes in savings a function of age-wealth profiles and thus indirectly of the amount invested in human capital.

A lifetime consumption pattern is assumed to depend upon utility functions, expectations about earnings and other income, market interest rates, and planned bequests. Since savings are residually defined as the difference between income and consumption, savings are adjusted over a lifetime so as to make the consumption plan feasible. In particular, since earnings are high during the middle ages and low during the younger ages and retirement, the rate of savings would also be high during the middle ages and low or even

26 See section 5 of Appendix B for a more general result.

27 See especially Friedman, *Consumption Function.*

28 This approach to life-cycle consumption patterns has been stressed by F. Modigliani and his associates. See Modigliani and Brumberg, in *Post-Keynesian Economics,* or F. Modigliani and A. Ando, "The Life Cycle Hypothesis of Savings," *American Economic Review,* March 1963.

negative during other periods. Broadly speaking, this pattern is usually found in empirical studies.[29]

More precise implications can be obtained by specifying the model more fully. In order to bring out clearly and simply the effects of human capital, several assumptions will be added that certainly have to be modified in a more complete analysis. Thus, let it be assumed that each cohort knows its earnings profile, that a single market interest rate applies to all transactions, that consumption is the same at all ages, and that after entry into the labor force the nonhuman wealth of a cohort can be changed only by its own savings and dissavings.[30] Each cohort starts out with wealth, partly in earning power and partly in property, and at "its" death leaves behind wealth, partly in the earning power of descendants and other subsequent cohorts and partly in property.

If its bequest, or terminal wealth, equaled the amount it was bequested, or initial wealth—i.e., if there were zero generational or "social" savings—the rate of savings[31] at any age would exactly equal the rate of change of human wealth.[32] So savings would be negative from the initial to the peak human-wealth age, zero then,[33] positive at subsequent ages until retirement, and zero during retirement. A more reasonable assumption for the United States and other developed economies would be that social savings were positive, or that terminal wealth exceeded initial wealth. Then the initial dissavings would be smaller and of shorter duration, the zero savings rate would be reached before the peak wealth age, and a positive savings rate would continue into the retirement period.

Since the wealth profile of unskilled workers would decline continuously, they would have positive savings throughout their labor force period. Profiles of workers with investment in human capital,

---

[29] See Friedman, *Consumption Function,* Tables 8 and 9, and F. Modigliani and A. Ando, "The 'Permanent Income' and the 'Life Cycle' Hypothesis of Saving Behavior: Comparison and Tests" in *Consumption and Saving,* I. Friend and R. Jones, eds., Vol. II, Philadelphia, 1960, Table III-4.

[30] These assumptions, as well as several others, are also made by Modigliani *et al.* in their quantitative work.

[31] Note that our concept of savings, unlike the usual ones, includes investment in the human capital of subsequent generations as well as accumulation of assets.

[32] In terms of the language just used, savings would equal the rate of depreciation or appreciation on wealth.

[33] Before retirement, only at the peak wealth age would permanent income, defined as the income accruing on wealth, equal actual income. So depreciation and thus savings equal zero when actual and permanent incomes are equal.

on the other hand, rise initially more sharply and longer, the greater the investment. So the magnitude and extent of the initial dissavings would be greater for cohorts with more human capital.

Since an initial period of dissavings would result in an initial decline in nonhuman capital, an increase in indebtedness, or some of both,[34] the large secular increase in human capital should have caused a secular increase in household indebtedness. Therefore, the observed increase in consumer credit and other debt may not have resulted simply from an increased demand for durables or from improvements in the market for credit, but probably also was a disguised effect of the secular increase in education and other human capital.

A change in the rate of population growth would probably change aggregate, although not necessarily social, savings because the relative number of persons at different ages would be affected. If savings rates were always greater at younger than at older ages, an increase in population growth would increase the aggregate savings rate. Such would tend to be the result in a world of unskilled workers because they would save more throughout the labor force period than during retirement.[35] Skilled workers, on the other hand, would have low and even negative savings rates at the youngest ages, and a larger population growth rate might actually reduce their aggregate savings rate. Therefore, the secular increase in human capital should have reduced the positive effect of a higher population growth rate on aggregate savings, and might even have led to a negative effect.

[34] Consequently, one can say that investment in human capital is substituted for investment in other capital.

[35] This essentially is the model assumed by Kuznets in his discussion of the effect of population growth on aggregate savings. See his *Capital in the American Economy: Its Formation and Financing,* Princeton for NBER, 1961, Chapter III. Also see Modigliani and Ando in *American Economic Review,* March 1963, pp. 59-60.

CHAPTER VIII

Summary and Conclusions

---

1. Summary

Most investments in human capital—e.g., formal education, on-the-job training, or migration—raise observed earnings at older ages, because returns are part of earnings then, and lower them at younger ages, because costs are deducted from earnings at that time. Since these common effects are produced by very different kinds of investment in human capital, a basis is provided for a unified and comprehensive theory. The analysis in Part One starts with a discussion of specific kinds of human capital, with the most attention paid to on-the-job training, because the latter clearly illustrates and emphasizes the common effects. This leads to a general theory applying to any kind of human capital.

The general theory has a wide variety of important applications. It helps to explain such diverse phenomena as interpersonal and interarea differences in earnings, the shape of age-earnings profiles— the relation between age and earnings—and the effect of specialization on skill. For example, because observed earnings are gross of the return on human capital, some persons earn more than others simply because they invest more in themselves. Because "abler" persons tend to invest more than others, the distribution of earnings would be very unequal and skewed even if "ability" were symmetrically and not too unequally distributed. Further, the conventional practice of adding returns to and subtracting costs from earnings serves to steepen age-earnings profiles and to increase their concavity as investment in human capital increases. Still another example, learning on and off the job has the same kind of effects on observed earnings as formal education, training, and other recognized investments in human capital, and can be considered one way to invest in human capital. Because all such activities have similar effects on earnings, the total amount invested in human capital, and rates of return on this investment can, on certain reasonable assumptions, be estimated from information on observed earnings alone.

Some investments in human capital do not affect earnings because costs are paid and returns are collected not by the persons involved but by the firms, industries, or countries employing them. These investments, which are called "specific" investments, range from hiring costs to executive training and are of considerable importance. They help to explain the well-known fact that unemployment is greater among unskilled than skilled workers in the United States, for more specific capital is invested in the latter and employers have special incentive to continue them on the payroll. Similarly, incompletely vested pension plans may be used because they help to insure firms against a loss on their specific investment. The analysis further suggests that this type of investment is relatively more important in monopsonistic than in competitive firms.

Part Two investigates empirically the effect of one kind of human capital—formal education—on earnings and productivity in the United States. The basic technique used is to adjust data on the earnings or incomes of persons with different amounts of education for other relevant differences between them. Chapter IV determines the relation in recent years between earnings and college education, considering, among other things, college costs and the greater "ability" of college persons. The rate of return to an average college entrant is considerable, of the order of 10 or 12 per cent per annum; the rate is higher to urban, white, male college graduates and lower to college drop-outs, nonwhites, women, and rural persons. Differences in the relative number of, say, white and nonwhite or urban and rural high-school graduates who go to college are consistent with the differences in their rates of return.

General observation indicates that college graduates tend to be more "able" than high-school graduates, apart from the effect of college education. This is indicated also by information gathered on I.Q., rank in class, father's education or income, physical health, ability to communicate, and several other distinguishing characteristics. A few studies permit some assessment of the relative importance of ability and education in explaining earning differentials between college and high-school persons. By and large, it appears, ability explains only a relatively small part of the differentials and college education explains the larger part. Apparently, moreover, the rate of return from college is positively related to the level of ability since there is evidence that ability plays a larger part in determining the earnings of college than high-school persons.

Gains from college education vary not only between groups, like men and women, but also substantially within given groups. Indeed, some calculations in Chapter IV indicate that the dispersion of rates of return among white male college graduates is as large as, and perhaps larger than, the very considerable dispersion in the returns per dollar of capital among smaller corporate manufacturing firms. A large dispersion makes it difficult for any individual to anticipate his gain from education, a difficulty that is compounded by a pay-off period of some twenty to twenty-five years. This long pay-off period provides an economic justification for flexible or "liberal" education since most of the benefits would be received when the economic environment was greatly different from that prevailing at the time of entry into the labor force.

In Chapter V attention is focused on the social gain from college education as measured by its effects on national productivity. The major difficulty here, one that always plagues economists, is in measuring the benefits and costs to society that are not captured or borne by college-educated persons. All that could be done was to derive—on the basis of crude information—lower and what is best labeled "possible" upper limits to the social rates of return, limits that unfortunately are wide apart. The more reliable lower limits thus derived do not differ much from the private rates of return, but the upper levels are almost double the latter. In the same chapter it is shown that private rates of return on college education exceed those on business capital. The evidence is insufficient to decide whether this, or the converse, is true of the social rates.

Chapter VI estimates private rates of return from high-school education. Before adjusting for differential ability, these private rates from high-school turn out to be greater than those from college. But the "true" rates, after adjustment for ability, may not be, for ability apparently differs more between high-school and elementary-school students than between college and high-school students. A similar qualification applies to the crude evidence indicating that rates on elementary-school education are the highest of all.

Summary and Conclusions

A traditional view among economists—certainly the dominant one when I was a graduate student—is that changes in educational attainments have been largely autonomous, and that the secular increase in education has caused a decline in earning differentials and rates of return on education. Such evidence as there is, presented in Chapter VI, suggests indeed that the relative position of high-school and college graduates probably declined during the first forty years of the century under the impact of increases in their numbers. But the evidence is scattered and much less reliable than the information available for the past twenty years. The latter, presented in the same chapter, indicates that the rapid growth in the number of high-school and college graduates has not reduced their economic position. An alternative view, supported by this evidence, has therefore gained many adherents in recent years; namely, that educational attainments in good part adjust to, as well as influence, the demands of the economic system.

Chapter VII shows that investment in education in fact steepens and increases the concavity of age-earnings profiles, as predicted by the theory in Part One. Partly as an aside, the discussion also includes a critical examination of the common belief that earnings tend to turn down when persons reach their late forties or fifties; this belief is shown to be founded on an illusion, for it is based on data that do not take economic progress into account. The same chapter shows that the steepness of age-wealth profiles—the relation between age and the discounted value of subsequent earnings—is also increased by investment in education and other human capital. It is suggested that the apparent large secular increase in the peak wealth age in the United States resulted from a secular increase in the amount invested in such capital. The chapter concludes with some applications of these profiles, especially to life-cycle changes in savings, indebtedness, and consumption.

2. Future Research

I have no illusions that this study has more than scratched the surface of the research required on the economic effects of education and other investments in human capital. There is need for additional research on many different aspects of the gain from education and on other implications of the theoretical analysis in Part One. A few examples of possible research will be briefly mentioned.

Summary and Conclusions

Economists have been surprisingly ignorant of the quantitative effects of different kinds of ability on earnings and productivity, yet such knowledge is essential in estimating the gains from investment in human capital (and in resolving many other problems as well). The surveys utilized in this study show the feasibility and importance of determining these effects, and many more such attempts should be made in the future.

Only a limited amount could be said about the social gains from education because of ignorance about the external effects. This ignorance is closely connected with ignorance about the "residual" in calculations of the contribution of various factors to growth. Little progress can be achieved, therefore, in improving the estimation of these social gains until methods are discovered for reducing the residual.

To many underdeveloped countries the gains from education in the United States fifty years ago may be more relevant than the gains today because this country was much poorer then and many fewer persons were educated. The evidence available indicates a decline in the private gain from high-school and college education in the first forty years of the century, but a much more intensive study is required because this evidence is not very reliable. Fortunately, Albert Fishlow has already begun a study for the National Bureau of historical changes in the demand for and supply of educated persons in the United States, and his study will throw considerably more light on trends in the gains from education.

I have not tried to estimate gains to persons taking specialized programs in high school and college. Some literature is already available on the gains to various professionals, such as doctors, lawyers, engineers, or scientists,[1] and additional comparisons can and should be made between persons with B.A., M.A., or Ph.D. degrees, liberal arts or more specialized college majors, commercial or academic high-school programs, and so on. My estimates of the average gains to high-school and college persons would be useful as a yardstick to determine when gains were unusually large or small; for example, since average gains are large, the gains from particular specialties

---

[1] See, for example, M. Friedman and S. Kuznets, *Income from Independent Professional Practice*, New York, NBER, 1945; G. J. Stigler and D. Blank, *The Demand and Supply of Scientific Personnel*, New York, NBER, 1957; or W. L. Hansen, "The 'Shortage' of Engineers," *Review of Economics and Statistics*, August 1961.

would have to be very large before they could be considered "excessive."[2]

There has been persistent interest, if little success, in measuring the differences in quality among high schools and colleges. One way to measure quality within an economic context is to relate expenditures on students and other variables in different schools to the (ability-adjusted) incomes of their graduates.[3] Such studies have already been undertaken on a small sample basis,[4] and, with sufficient persistence, additional information could be collected to expand the samples considerably.

Chapter VII presents empirical work dealing with other implications of the theory outlined in Part One, such as the shape of age-earnings and age-wealth profiles, differential unemployment, turnover of military personnel, differential pay of school teachers, and estimates of the amount invested in human capital. The theory is so rich in implications that many more could be investigated, and empirical work has already begun relating human capital to the turnover in employment of women, comparative advantage and United States exports, the elasticity of substitution between labor and physical capital, and several other problems.

Probably the most important application is to differences in incomes between regions and countries, either over time or cross-sectionally at a moment in time. The estimates presented here of the gains from education could be used to improve Denison's estimates of the contribution of education to economic growth in the United States. The major improvement, however, must await additional work on the external effects of education, work that, I fear, will be rather slow in coming.

[2] This yardstick has been applied by H. G. Lewis to the medical profession with extremely interesting and surprising results: the rate of return to doctors (on their additional training compared to dentists) has apparently been no higher and perhaps lower than that to all college graduates. See his *Unionism and Relative Wages in the United States: An Empirical Inquiry*, Chicago, 1963.

[3] Another approach is from the cost side, and relates differences in expenditures to differences in curriculum, size, teaching staff, and other "real" inputs; in technical language, this approach in effect constructs "hedonic" cost indexes. An interesting initial study along these lines has been made by R. Calkins, "The Unit Costs of Programs in Higher Education," unpublished Ph.D. dissertation, Columbia University, 1963.

[4] See, e.g., the study by S. Hunt discussed in Chapter IV, "Income Determinants for College Graduates and the Return to Educational Investments," unpublished Ph.D. dissertation, Yale University, 1963.

Summary and Conclusions

A more immediate, and also important, application is to the personal distribution of incomes. This field has been afflicted with numerous theories that scarcely go beyond the skewness in the over-all distribution of incomes although substantial empirical material on the anatomy of income distribution has been accumulated. The theory developed in section 3 of Chapter III combines the effects of investment in human capital and differential ability, and, unlike other theories, contains many implications about income distribution. The empirical work of Mincer, referred to earlier, as well as the fact that at least three-fifths of earnings are attributable either to investment in human capital or to differential ability,[5] is suggestive of the promise offered by this approach. I hope to present further work along these lines in the not too distant future.

3. Concluding Comments

In recent years the outpouring of work on education and other types of human capital has reached such a level that some persons have scornfully rejected it as simply another fad, while others have been repelled by a few reckless applications and by its use to justify all kinds of public policies. To those who believe in the great value of the concept, the excesses have been most unfortunate, although perhaps unavoidable. Probably no important development has ever sailed smoothly into the mainstream of economic thought.

One might, nevertheless, get discouraged were it not for the fact that peoples of the world differ enormously in productivity, that these differences are in turn largely related to environmental factors, and that the latter are in turn related to the accumulation of knowledge and the maintenance of health. The concept of investment in human capital simply organizes and stresses these basic truths. Perhaps they are obvious, but obvious truths can be extremely important. Indeed, I would venture the judgment that human capital is going to be an important part of the thinking about development, income distribution, labor turnover, and many other problems for a long time to come.

[5] Estimated by taking one minus the ratio of the average earnings of persons with no education to the average earnings of all persons.

APPENDIX A

Sources and Methods

THIS appendix sets out some of the sources and methods used in deriving the rates of return and other figures presented in the study. It should be read by all persons planning to use the findings since the basic data are quite imperfect and many adjustments could have been made differently. First, the methods used to estimate incomes at different levels of education are presented and then those used to estimate costs.

1. Incomes

A. THE BASIC DATA

The basic income data came from the 1940 and 1950 Censuses and from the surveys of 1956 and 1958.[1] M. Zeman estimated mean earnings by age and education in 1939 from data in the 1940 Census which gave the distribution of persons by income class.[2] I used the 1950 Census to make my own estimates of incomes in 1949, and H. Miller estimated means from the 1956 and 1958 surveys.[3] Zeman used

[1] See *Sixteenth Census of the United States: 1940, Population, Education, Educational Attainment by Economic Characteristics and Marital Status*, Bureau of the Census, Washington, 1947, Tables 29 and 31. *United States Census of Population, 1950*, Special Reports, *Education*, Vol. IV, part 5, Chapter B, Bureau of the Census, Washington, 1953, Table 12. *Income of Families and Persons in the United States* for 1956 and 1958, Current Population Reports, Consumer Income, Bureau of the Census, Series P-60, nos. 27 and 33, Washington, 1958 and 1960.

[2] See his "A Quantitative Analysis of White-Non-White Income Differentials in the United States in 1939," unpublished Ph.D. dissertation, University of Chicago, 1955, Tables 13 and 16.

[3] See his "Annual and Lifetime Income in Relation to Education, 1939-1959," *American Economic Review*, December 1960, Table 1.

incomes near the midpoints of all closed income classes as the means of these classes, and Lorenz distributions to estimate the means of the $5,000-and-over class. Miller used the midpoints of all closed classes and the single figure $20,000 as the mean of the $10,000-and-over class. I used essentially the midpoints of all closed classes and Pareto distributions to estimate means in the open-end class, except that the maximum mean in the open-end class was limited to $27,000, the minimum to $15,000, and obviously incorrect figures were eliminated. The same means were used for elementary-school graduates as for high-school graduates.[4] These estimates are shown in Table A-1.

TABLE A-1

OPEN–END MEANS USED IN CALCULATING 1949 INCOMES
(dollars)

Age	Years of Education			
	8	12	13–15	16+
14–15	15,000	--	--	--
16–17	15,000	--	--	--
18–19	15,000	15,000	--	--
20–21	15,000	15,000	15,000	--
22–24	15,000	15,000	15,000	16,826
25–29	15,213	15,213	15,068	17,157
30–34	15,782	15,782	15,915	16,926
35–44	17,971	17,971	19,231	22,349
45–54	22,739	22,739	25,446	27,000
55–64	26,656	26,656	27,000	27,000

Source: See text.

My estimates for 1949 differ from those of Houthakker and Miller[5] primarily because of the different treatment of the open-end class. They use the same open-end mean at all age and educational levels, Miller $20,000 and Houthakker $22,000, while mine rises significantly with age and education. There is little question that actual open-end means do rise with age and education, so that they overestimate incomes at lower levels relative to those at higher ones. Table A-2 indicates, however, that at most ages all three studies show similar income differentials between education classes. Zeman and Miller exclude persons with no income although they should be included in estimat-

[4] So few elementary-school graduates are in the open-end class that estimates based on Pareto distributions were unstable. Moreover, because so few are in this class, it does not greatly matter which means are used.

[5] *Ibid.* and H. S. Houthakker, "Education and Income," *Review of Economics and Statistics,* February 1959, pp. 24-28.

ing cohort incomes for exactly the same reason that dead members of a cohort are included (via mortality adjustments).

I have assumed that persons attend college only from ages 18 to 22½ and high school only 14 to 17. Actually, of course, high school and college are also attended at earlier and, especially after World War II, later ages. Moreover, the Census only tries to ascertain the highest grade completed and excludes partial years of schooling.

TABLE A-2

THREE ESTIMATES OF BEFORE-TAX INCOME DIFFERENTIALS
BETWEEN EDUCATION CLASSES IN 1949
(dollars)

	INCOME DIFFERENCES BETWEEN PERSONS WITH:					
	12 and 8 Years of School			16+ and 12 Years of School		
Age	Houthakker	Miller	Becker[a]	Houthakker	Miller	Becker[a]
22-24	417		413	-522		-378
25-29	642	706	638	201	876	228
30-34	819		810	1,577		1,439
35-44	1,023	1,026	993	3,135	3,030	3,416
45-54	1,438	1,442	1,551	3,631	3,427	4,753
55-64	1,504	1,538	1,890	3,280	3,107	4,051

Source: Houthakker, Review of Economics and Statistics, February 1959, Table 1, p. 25; and Miller, American Economic Review, December 1960, Table 1, p. 966.
[a]Whites only.

Together, these facts imply that some persons over age 22½ with 16+ years of schooling would still be in school and, therefore, at best working only part time; similarly, for high-school graduates over age 18 and those with 13-15 years of school over age 20. Consequently, reported incomes at certain ages would not completely measure full-time incomes; data on the fraction of persons reporting no income, shown in Table A-3, suggest that in 1949 the bias is significant for 16+ years of schooling at ages 22-29, for 13-15 years at ages 20-24, for 12 years at ages 18-21, for 9-11 years at ages 16-19, and for 8 years at ages 14-17, while of lesser significance at other ages. Therefore, all persons with zero income have been included at these other ages, while only 2 per cent of persons who have 16+ school years aged 22-29, 13-15 years aged 20-24, and 12 years aged 18-21 are assumed to have no income (persons aged 14-19 with 8 and 9-11 years of schooling are discussed later).

Appendix A

B. UNDER- AND OVERREPORTING

From a comparison of Census and national income data, S. Goldsmith concluded that the Census underreports all types of income, the bias being greatest for dividends, interest, and other kinds of property income, and least for wages and salaries.[6] Her study suggests that wages and salaries were underreported by about 10 per cent. The 1940 data cover only wages and salaries, so they were simply uniformly

TABLE A-3

FRACTION OF WHITE MALES REPORTING NO INCOME
IN 1949 BY AGE AND EDUCATION CLASS

Age	Years of Education				
	8 (1)	9-11 (2)	12 (3)	13-15 (4)	16+ (5)
14-15	.778	--	--	--	--
16-17	.569	.595	--	--	--
18-19	.227	.333	.239	--	--
20-21	.129	.108	.102	.240	--
22-24	.065	.046	.052	.116	.123
25-29	.043	.030	.026	.046	.045
30-34	.035	.024	.020	.019	.022
35-44	.033	.025	.023	.020	.020
45-54	.041	.036	.035	.029	.025
55-64	.065	.060	.059	.046	.041

Source: 1950 Census of Population, Education, Vol. II, Table 12.

increased by 10 per cent to correct for the apparent Census bias. Since the understatement is probably greater at higher earning levels, the adjustment is probably too large at lower age-education classes and too small at upper classes.

To increase comparability with the 1940 Census, property incomes in the 1950 Census and the two Census surveys should be excluded. Since Table A-4 indicates, however, that aggregate earnings are about equal to the total incomes reported by the Census, the underreporting of earnings just about offsets the inclusion of property and other "unearned" income. Therefore, at the aggregate level at least, Census incomes can be used to measure true earnings. Although property income would be a larger percentage of total incomes at higher age-education levels, as noted above, the underreporting of earnings

[6] See Selma Goldsmith, "The Relation of Census Income Distribution Statistics to Other Income Data," *An Appraisal of the 1950 Census Income Data,* Studies in Income and Wealth 23, Princeton for NBER, 1958.

TABLE A-4

COMPARISON OF INCOMES REPORTED BY CENSUS
AND COMMERCE FOR 1946 AND 1954
(dollars)

Source and Type of Information	1946	1954
Total earnings		
OBE series, adjusted	135.1	218.8
Total income		
CPS	129.8	217.7

Source: S. Goldsmith, in Appraisal of 1950 Census
Income Data, Table 2.

probably also rises with age and education. Hence the unadjusted data may not greatly overestimate earning differentials between different levels.

C. UNEMPLOYMENT

Earnings of less-educated persons are usually more affected by business cycles, partly because their employment is more volatile and partly because wages fluctuate more than salaries. Incomes reported in Census and other surveys refer to particular stages of business cycles, while rates of return depend on lifetime earnings accruing over several full cycles. The 1950 Census and the 1956 and 1958 surveys cover relatively normal times and are probably only slightly affected, but the 1940 Census covers a period of sizable unemployment and might be seriously biased. Accordingly, I have tried to correct the 1940 Census data for their departure from "normality."

First, the average unemployment rate of wage and salary workers was estimated for each educational level in 1940, and the average duration of unemployment of all persons unemployed less than a year was computed.[7] If the average duration did not depend on education and if unemployed persons earned the same when employed as others, one could estimate what earnings would have been if nobody were unemployed.[8] Column 3 of Table A-5 presents these estimates which show that unemployment did increase percentage earning differentials between educational levels.

[7] Persons unemployed more than a year presumably do not have any wages or salaries and, therefore, are already excluded from Zeman's figures.

[8] Actually only abnormal unemployment should be eliminated as unemployment is normally also higher among less-educated persons. Only a small bias results, however, because normal unemployment was a small part of the total in 1939.

TABLE A-5

ADJUSTMENT FOR UNEMPLOYMENT IN 1939 BY EDUCATION CLASS

Education (years)	Per Cent Unemployed (wage and salary workers) (1)	Duration of Unemployment (years) (2)	Employment Adjustment (3)	Earnings Adjustment (4)
7-8	20.37	.63	1.08	1.08
12	14.10	.63	1.06	1.08
13-15	10.54	.63	1.04	1.07
16+	5.92	.63	1.02	1.07

Source

Col. 1: 1940 Census of Population, Education, Table 17, p. 76.
Col. 2: Computed from 1940 Census of Population, The Labor Force (Sample Statistics), Occupational Characteristics, Washington, 1943, Table 17, pp. 199 and 202.
Col. 4: Based on figures in ibid., Tables 3 and 6; and Employment, Payroll, Hours and Earnings, Bureau of Labor Statistics, L.S. 53-2884 and L.S. 53-0902.

Deviations of actual wages and actual salaries in 1939 from "normal" levels were determined by assuming that normal levels in 1939 equaled a simple average of actual levels from 1937 to 1941. Wage earners were separated from salary earners at each educational level with the help of Census information. If actual wages and salaries deviated from normal values by the same percentage at each educational level, normal wages and salaries in 1939 could then be easily determined. Ratios of normal to actual values are shown in column 4.

The coefficients in columns 3 and 4 were applied uniformly to all age classes, even though the incidence, at least of unemployment, is greater at younger ages. Although earnings of less-educated persons were raised by relatively large percentages, they were not raised by relatively large absolute amounts because the level of earnings is positively related to education. Accordingly, the adjustments for the depressed conditions of 1939 had a surprisingly small effect on rates of return.

D. COVERAGE IN 1939

The 1940 Census only reports the incomes of native whites with less than $50 of income other than wages and salaries. About one-third of all whites and more than half of the college graduates are omitted. The latter are especially underrepresented because independent professionals are excluded and most of them are college graduates. To rectify this underrepresentation, I estimated separately the earnings and number at different ages of independent dentists, lawyers, and physicians.

Table A-6 presents these estimates along with the earnings and number of college graduates computed from the Census. The relative number and earnings of independent professionals rise strongly with age. Column 5 presents estimates of the average earnings of both groups combined, which are weighted averages of the earnings of each, the weights being their relative numbers. A comparison of columns 3 and 5 shows that the combined average is not very different from the Census average before age class 45-54. Since rates of return are dominated by earnings at younger ages, the omission of independent professionals would have little effect on these rates: it would lower the rate to college graduates by less than 1 percentage point.

Although the inclusion of independent professionals increases the coverage of college graduates to about the same levels as other education classes, considerable biases might result since more than one-third of all whites are still excluded. The biases offset each other to some extent, however, because presumably foreign-born persons earn less than natives and natives with property income earn more than other natives. Probably the net effect is to lower rates of return from high-school and college education since the relative importance of the foreign born is smaller at higher educational levels. Fortunately, as Table A-7 suggests, the biases are probably not very large because

TABLE A-6

AVERAGE EARNINGS OF CENSUS COLLEGE GRADUATES
AND INDEPENDENT DOCTORS, DENTISTS, AND LAWYERS IN 1939

	Independent Professionals		Census College Graduates		Earnings of Both Groups Combined (dollars)
			Earnings (adjusted for unemployment)		
Age	Earnings (dollars)	Number	(dollars)	Number	
	(1)	(2)	(3)	(4)	(5)
25-29	2,174	15,631	1,997	177,400	2,011
30-34	3,285	38,762	2,878	161,800	2,957
35-44	4,491	108,476	3,782	187,060	4,042
45-54	5,028	72,278	4,185	97,920	4,543
55-64	4,238	45,690	3,782	42,120	4,019

Source: Cols. 1 and 2 computed from William Weinfeld, "Income of Physicians 1929-49," Survey of Current Business, July 1951, Tables 1 and 16; "Income of Lawyers, 1929-49," Survey of Current Business, August 1949, Tables 1 and 10; and "Income of Dentists 1929-48," Survey of Current Business, January 1950, Tables 2 and 9; cols. 3 and 4 from 1940 Census of Population, Education.

the relative number of persons excluded is much smaller at younger ages for all education classes.

E. TAXES

Census and other surveys report before-tax incomes whereas incomes net of direct personal taxes are needed to estimate private rates of return. Internal revenue data were used in 1949 to find the average fraction paid in taxes at each income class, including the open-end class.[9] Means of after-tax incomes at all age-education levels were

TABLE A-7

FRACTION OF NATIVE WHITES AND URBAN WHITES INCLUDED IN 1939 DATA, BY AGE AND EDUCATION

Age	Ratio of Native Whites Included and Independent Professionals to All Native Whites, by Years of Education				Ratio of Urban White Males Included[a] to All Urban White Males, by Years of Education			
	7-8 (1)	12 (2)	13-15 (3)	16+ (4)	7-8 (5)	12 (6)	13-15 (7)	16+ (8)
18-19	.964	.758	.490	.582	--	--	--	--
20-21	.826	.850	.636	.589	.705	.740	.479	.495
22-24	.840	.863	.757	.696				
25-29	.843	.841	.795	.754	.728	.773	.724	.675
30-34	.822	.798	.745	.785	.671	.720	.675	.717
35-44	.776	.718	.651	.836	.589	.606	.570	.718
45-54	.704	.621	.553	.742	.488	.491	.480	.612
55-64	.604	.521	.443	.698	.386	.395	.369	.549

Source: Numerators are from Table A-6 and sources cited there; denominators of cols. 1, 2, and 4 are from <u>1940 Census of Population, Education,</u> Table 29, pp. 14 f; denominators of cols. 5, 6, 7, and 8 are from <u>1940 Census of Population,</u> Vol. IV: Characteristics by Age, Part 1 (U.S. Summary), Washington, 1943, Table 18, pp. 78 and 81.

[a]Also includes rural independent professionals aged 25 and over.

estimated from the after-tax incomes in each income class. Although there was little change in tax schedules between 1949 and 1956-58, the fraction of income paid in taxes increased from 7.5 to over 10 per cent between 1949 and 1956 because of the growth in money incomes. At each age-education class the fraction of income taxed in 1956 and 1958 was assumed to equal the fraction taxed in 1949 multiplied by the ratio of the aggregate tax rates. A more sophisticated adjustment would not have much effect on the results.

[9] See *Statistics of Income for 1949,* Part I, Washington, 1954, Table 8. The separate returns for women were excluded.

Only about 1.5 per cent of income was paid in direct personal taxes in 1939.[10] Urban males with seven or more years of schooling presumably paid a somewhat larger fraction: native whites perhaps about 4 per cent and nonwhites about 2 per cent. As mentioned in Chapter IV, 1939 cohorts receive the bulk of their incomes not in 1939 but in the 1940's, 1950's, and 1960's, and would be subject to the higher rates prevailing then. The after-tax incomes of 1939 cohorts were also estimated assuming that they paid the same fraction in taxes at each age-education level as 1949 cohorts did.

F. URBAN-RURAL DISTRIBUTION

The 1940 Census covers all urban persons while the other surveys cover rural persons as well. If elementary, high-school, and college graduates were differently distributed by place of residence, the rates of return could be biased since money incomes are related to size of place of residence. Table A-8 indicates that they had about the same distribution among urban areas; more educated persons, however,

TABLE A-8

DISTRIBUTION OF PERSONS OF DIFFERENT EDUCATIONAL LEVELS
BY SIZE OF PLACE OF RESIDENCE, 1939

Years of Education	Urban Population (per cent)			Urban as Per Cent of Total (4)
	Over 250,000 (1)	25,000–250,000 (2)	2,500–25,000 (3)	
7–8	40.6	29.6	29.8	50.1
12	37.3	32.5	30.2	66.9
16+	39.1	30.9	30.1	76.4

Source: Cols. 1–3 from Table 17; col. 4 from 1940 Census of Population, Education, Table 29, pp. 147–151.

were less likely to live in rural areas. Consequently, the rates would have an upward bias in 1949 and later years because rural incomes are lower than urban ones even when education is held constant. The bias is small, however, because relatively few persons between the crucial ages of 18 and 45 are in nonurban areas.

[10] Taxes paid were found in *Statistics of Income for 1939*, Part I, Washington, 1942; adjusted gross income was estimated by C. H. Kahn, *Business and Professional Income Under the Personal Income Tax*, Princeton for NBER, 1964, Chapter 5.

G. HOURS OF WORK

Hours of work may differ among education classes for a variety of reasons: some persons retire earlier, have the opportunity to work more hours during any week, take longer vacations, and so on. Perhaps rates of return should be estimated from earnings per hour rather than the annual earnings presented in the Census and other reports. Fortunately, this difficult question does not have to be answered since average weekly hours of work apparently do not vary greatly among education classes. Table A-9 presents estimates from the 1940 Census based on the assumption that within occupations average hours of work did not vary systematically by education. In a recently published study, Finegan also finds no significant relation between hours of work and education.[11]

TABLE A-9

AVERAGE HOURS WORKED IN 1939, BY EDUCATIONAL LEVEL

Years of Education	Average Hours Worked
9–11	44.0
12	44.5
13–15	45.1
16+	44.7

Source: <u>1940 Census of Population, Labor Force (Sample Statistics), Occupational Characteristics,</u> Table 3 (all employed persons) and Table 9 (wage and salary workers only).

2. Costs

A. EARNINGS OF STUDENTS

Earnings of students cannot be estimated directly from the Census reports since these do not separate student earnings from those of full-time participants in the labor force with the same number of completed school years. If "full-time" students spend three-quarters of the available working time at school and, therefore, have one-quarter (summers) available for employment, the simplest assumption is that they could earn about one-quarter of what they would earn if they were not attending school. That this is a surprisingly good assumption is brought out by Table A-10, which presents three largely

11 A. Finegan, "A Cross-Sectional Analysis of Hours of Work," *Journal of Political Economy,* October 1962. He does find a relation when income is held constant.

independent estimates of the earnings of college students. The first simply assumes that they earn one-quarter of the earnings of high-school graduates aged 18-21; the second comes from a study giving the earnings of a sample of college students during the academic year 1952-53; the third is based partly on this sample and largely on the actual labor force participation of nonstudents and students between age 18 and 24. The last estimate indicates that college students work about one-quarter as much as nonstudents of the same age, while a comparison of the first and second estimates suggests that they earn about one-quarter as much as high-school graduates of the same age.[12]

TABLE A-10

ALTERNATIVE ESTIMATES OF FRACTION OF EARNINGS OF HIGH-SCHOOL
GRADUATES OF SAME AGE RECEIVED BY COLLEGE STUDENTS

Source of Estimate	Fraction
Becker	.250
Costs of attending college	.349
Labor force participation	.236

Source: The denominator of the second estimate is my estimate of the average earnings of high-school graduates aged 18-21 in 1949; the numerator is determined from Costs of Attending College, Table 8, p. 48. The third estimate is largely derived from "The Employment of Students, October 1960," in Monthly Labor Review, July 1961, Tables C and E. Since the labor force participation surveys were taken in October, they tend to understate the relative participation of college students because they participate more during the summer. I have assumed that the relative participation of college students during the summer is the same as their relative earnings during the summer (derived from Costs of Attending College, Table 8), while the participation of nonstudents is the same throughout the year. The over-all participation rate of college students relative to nonstudents aged 18-24 could then be estimated from the formula

$$p = \frac{3}{4} s + \frac{1}{4} (3r)s,$$

where p is their over-all relative participation, s is their relative participation during the nonsummer months, and $3r$ is the participation of college students during the summer relative to the rest of the year. According to the sources cited, $3r = 1.413$ and $s = .214$; therefore $p = .236$.

12 The ratio is somewhat higher in the second estimate because the earnings of students (in the numerator) are based on the academic year 1952-53, while the earnings of high-school graduates (in the denominator) are based on 1949. An adjustment for the strong general rise in earnings between 1949 and 1952-53 would lower the ratio to about .29. The difference between .25 and .29 is probably explained by the fact that the average age of college students is somewhat greater than 20, and their average ability is greater than that of high-school graduates. The .25 estimate, in effect, adjusts costs for the differential ability of college students, while the .29 estimate does not.

Consequently, the assumption that college students earn about one-quarter of the amount earned by high-school graduates of the same age is apparently fairly accurate, probably more so than some subtler assumptions that have been used.[13]

The 1940 Census and the 1956 and 1958 surveys do not give the earnings of persons younger than 18, so I simply assumed that the average earnings of elementary-school graduates increase from ages 14 to 18 at the same rate as from ages 18 to 21. The 1950 Census does give the incomes of persons aged 14-17 classified by education level. Column 1 of Table A-11 presents the mean incomes at ages 14-15 and 16-17 of all persons who have completed eight years of schooling, while column 2 presents much higher estimates obtained by extrapolating the rate of increase between ages 18-19 and 20-21. Since the

TABLE A-11

ALTERNATIVE ESTIMATES OF EARNINGS OF PERSONS AGED 14-17 WITH
EIGHT YEARS OF SCHOOLING, 1949
(dollars)

Age	Including All Persons with Zero Incomes (1)	Extrapolated from Earnings at Age 18-19 and 20-21 (2)	Assuming Only 5 Per Cent Have Zero Incomes (3)
14-15	104	333	431
16-17	258	525	558

Source: 1950 Census of Population, Education, Table 12.

Census usually understates incomes immediately following the typical age of entrance into the labor force (see the earlier discussion in section 1a), most of those with zero incomes among college persons aged 20-29 and high-school persons aged 16-21 were omitted. Column 3 of Table A-11 gives the average incomes of elementary-school graduates

---

[13] Schultz' estimate of the earnings foregone by college students in 1950 is a good deal larger than that implicit in ours (see his "Capital Formation by Education," *Journal of Political Economy,* December 1960, Tables 1 and 2), partly because he uses the actual age distribution of college students and partly because he assumes (wrongly, I believe) that they forego forty weeks of income. (I am indebted to Schultz for very helpful discussions and correspondence on alternative estimating methods.) Blitz' estimates are even higher than Schultz' (see Rudolph C. Blitz, "A Calculation of Income Foregone by Students: Supplement to 'The Nation's Educational Outlay,' " in *Economics of Higher Education,* Selma J. Mushkin, ed., Washington, 1962, Appendix B, pp. 390-403). Albert Fishlow is currently making very detailed estimates of opportunity costs.

at ages 14-17 when zero incomes are assumed to be only 5 per cent of the total. These figures are actually higher than those based on extrapolation because about 78 per cent of 14- to 15-year-olds and 57 per cent of 16- to 17-year-olds with eight years of schooling reported no income in 1949. Yet less than 7 per cent of the elementary-school graduates over age 22 reported no income.[14]

The earnings of high-school students were assumed to equal one-quarter the estimated earnings of elementary-school graduates aged 14-17. Another estimate is presented in Table A-12 that is derived largely from surveys of labor force participation by students and nonstudents aged 14-17. This estimate indicates somewhat smaller actual, though larger foregone, earnings than ours does.[15]

TABLE A-12

ALTERNATIVE ESTIMATES OF FRACTION OF EARNINGS OF ELEMENTARY-
SCHOOL GRADUATES OF THE SAME AGE RECEIVED BY HIGH-SCHOOL STUDENTS

Source of Estimate	Fraction
Becker	.25
Labor force participation	.21

Source: The second estimate was obtained in the same way as the third estimate in Table A-10. The sources are Employment of Students, Current Population Reports, Labor Force, October 1955 (Series P-50, No. 64), Tables 1 and C; and Special Labor Force Report No. 16, "The Employment of Students, October 1960," Monthly Labor Review, July 1961, Tables C and E. I had to assume that the relative summer participation of high-school students was the same as that of college students.

B. DIRECT PRIVATE COSTS

Information on current expenditures, tuition, and enrollments for 1940 and 1950 were taken from a special study[16] rather than directly

14 Many of the persons who leave school after only completing the eighth grade were still in school at ages 14-15 and even 16-17 (see *School and Early Employment Experience of Youth,* Dept. of Labor, No. 1277, Washington, 1960, Tables 5-6). Moreover, the same study indicates that teen-agers not in school have a lot of "unexplained time," i.e., time when they were not in the labor force, in training, sick, etc. (see *ibid.,* Table 20). Possibly these considerations explain the extraordinarily large fraction reporting no income.

15 Schultz' estimates (*Journal of Political Economy,* December 1960, Table 5) of both actual and foregone earnings are again much larger than ours.

16 See *Current Operating Expenditures and Income of Higher Education in the United States, 1930, 1940 and 1950* (called *COEIHE* in later references), a Staff Technical Paper of the Commission on Financing Higher Education, Columbia University Press, New York, 1952, Tables 3, 58, 83, 91, and 115.

from the Biennial Surveys of the Office of Education because the study apparently presents more consistent and comparable data.[17] Information from the biennial surveys improved considerably during the 1950's and was used for 1956 and 1958.

Gross tuition and fees would equal reported tuition and fees plus contributions by the federal government to the tuition of veterans. An estimate of tuition paid for extension courses was subtracted since enrollment figures exclude extension students. The estimate assumed that extension tuition was the same fraction of all tuition as current expenditures on extension were of all current expenditures.[18]

The tuition paid by students would be lower than the tuition received by colleges because of scholarships from colleges and other sources. The 1952-53 national sample provides information on scholarships received from both sources: together they averaged about 20.7 per cent of tuition.[19]

Figures on enrollment usually include part-time along with full-time students, and accordingly overestimate the number of full-time equivalents. A special study in 1958 indicated that part-timers were about 24 per cent of all male college students.[20] If part-timers averaged about half the course load of full-timers (they probably averaged somewhat less),[21] the number of full-time equivalents would be about 88 per cent of the total enrollment. All the college enrollment figures, therefore, have been multiplied by 0.88.

All these adjustments transformed the crude figures into full-time tuition charges and payments for nonextension students; payments

17 See *ibid.,* Introduction, pp. iii to ix.

18 These ratios were .073 in 1939 and .053 in 1949 (see *ibid.,* Tables 3 and 91).

19 See *Costs of Attending College,* Table 8. Scholarships from colleges averaged about 13.9 per cent of tuition, which is close to the 12.5 per cent estimate for 1953-54 of John F. Meck (see his *Testimony Before the House Ways and Means Committee, 1958,* General Revenue Revisions, Vol. 78, 85th Congress, 2nd Session, Washington, 1958, p. 1065).

20 *Total Enrollment in Institutions of Higher Education, First Term, 1959-60,* Washington, 1962, Table 1.

21 According to some estimates, part-time undergraduate students average about two-sevenths and part-time graduate students about three-fifth of the load of full-timers; together they would average about one-third. For these estimates, see R. W. Wallers, "Statistics of Attendance in American Universities and College, 1949," *School and Society,* December 1949, and S. Mushkin and E. McLoone, *Student Higher Education: Expenditures and Sources of Income in 16 Selected States,* Washington, 1960.

were $112 per student in 1939, $228 in 1949, $209 in 1956,[22] and $242 in 1958, and charges averaged about 25 per cent higher because of college and other scholarships. In recent years the Office of Education surveyed the tuition charged full-time students in a large number of colleges, and found an average of $296 in 1956-57 and $319 in 1957-58.[23] This is generally consistent with my estimates for these years considering the bias in favor of more expensive schools in the Office of Education survey, and the slight upward biases in my estimates of full-time equivalents and extension tuition.

The 1952-53 survey gives the average outlay by college students on books and supplies, travel between home and school, and capital (e.g., typewriters) used in school work. These were assumed to be the only other private direct costs and to be the same fraction of tuition in other years as they were in 1952-53. In that year books and supplies were 22.5 per cent of tuition, travel 23.9 per cent, and capital 7 per cent.[24]

High-school tuition was set equal to zero. The other direct costs of high-school students—transportation, books, etc.—were estimated by assuming that the ratio of these costs to expenditure per student by high schools equaled one-half the observed ratio for college students. The use of one-half is quite arbitrary and perhaps a somewhat different ratio would be more justifiable. However, a considerable change in the values assumed for these other direct costs would not have much effect on the estimated rates of return from high school.

[22] The decline from 1949 to 1956 was quite unexpected, but turned out to be rather easily explained. While average tuition per student increased somewhat in private colleges, it decreased substantially in public ones, and the fraction of students in public colleges increased from .51 in 1949 to .56 in 1956. (See "Statistics of Higher Education: Receipts, Expenditures and Property, 1949-50," Section II of *Biennial Survey of Education in the United States, 1948-50,* Washington, 1952, Table 2, and "Statistics of Higher Education: Receipts, Expenditures and Property, 1955-56," Volume II of *Biennial Survey of Education in the U.S., 1954-56,* Washington, 1959, Table X; and *Statistical Abstract of the U.S.-1961,* Table 157.) Average tuition declined in the public institutions partly because the relative number of veterans declined and public institutions were sometimes permitted to charge veterans going to school under the G.I. Bill more than other students.

[23] W. Robert Bokelman, *Higher Education Planning and Management Data, 1957-58,* Washington, 1958, Table 34.

[24] See *Costs of Attending College,* Table 8. Ten per cent of the capital was assumed to be used up during a single school year. This assumption is discussed in the next section.

Appendix A

C. DIRECT SOCIAL COSTS

Direct social costs equal the sum of current educational expenditures, capital used up on education, and property taxes that would have been levied if schools were not tax-exempt. Educational expenditures are much smaller than total expenditures by schools, since schools are multiproduct institutions (especially at the college level) that do extension work, house and feed students, organize athletic contests, conduct research, and so on. I have excluded from the total what the biennial survey calls "noneducational" expenditures, extension, organized research, and expenditures on "organized activities relating to instructional departments." One might argue that some research and organized activities expenditures should be included since these directly benefit students and make it easier to acquire a good faculty. Expenditures on them were only about 13.6 per cent of other educational expenditures in 1939, but rose to 29 per cent in 1949.[25] Including these expenditures as educational costs would have lowered the estimated rate of return about .75 of a percentage point in 1949—a relatively small difference.

The amount of tangible capital per school was estimated from an unpublished study by Robert Rude.[26] Only 80 per cent of all colleges in his sample reported their capital, so his figure for college capital may be too low; but since those not reporting were quite small, the bias is probably not large. Capital per student was obtained by dividing the amount per school by the number of students per school. The fraction of all capital used on "noneducational" activities (extension, housing, etc.) is assumed to be the same as the fraction of all current expenditures on these activities. If "current" expenditures on research and other noneducational activities include an allowance for capital overhead, some of the capital used on noneducational activities would be subtracted twice.[27] About 37 and 48

25 See *COEIHE*, Tables 58 and 83.

26 See his unpublished manuscript, "Assets of Private Nonprofit Institutions in the United States, 1890-1948," National Bureau of Economic Research, 1954. There is evidence that Rude overestimated the relative value of land (see an unpublished discussion by Z. Griliches).

27 On the other hand, if the current expenditures on research and other "noneducational" activities do not include any allowances for current "overhead," some of the general administrative expenditures and other such "overhead" should be allotted to these activities and excluded from my figures. I did not, however, try to make any adjustment for this.

per cent of college capital in 1939 and 1949, respectively, was excluded from Rude's estimates.[28]

The Office of Education combines expenditures of high schools and elementary schools. The expenditures of each could be estimated from the formula

$$wX + (1 - w)\, \alpha X = Y,$$

if w and α were known, where X is the expenditure per student in high schools, Y is the combined expenditure per student, w is the fraction of students in high schools, and $1/\alpha$ is the ratio of expenditures per student in high schools to those in elementary schools. Now w is regularly reported and α is occasionally reported. For example, it was stated that $1/\alpha$ equaled about 1.74 in 1939-40,[29] and I have used this ratio to estimate X, the expenditure per high-school student. High-school capital was assumed to be the same fraction of the combined capital as it was of the combined expenditures. Finally, noneducational expenditures and capital were assumed to be the same fraction of high school as they were of the combined elementary- and high-school expenditures and capital.

The opportunity cost of capital used in education, which measures the rate of return on other capital plus the rate of depreciation on capital in education, was assumed to be 10 per cent of its value per annum. Usually, rates of interest rather than rates of return have been used in measuring opportunity costs, even though the latter seem more appropriate in determining social as well as private costs. In any case, the estimated opportunity cost of capital would not have been much lower if interest rates had been used.

Schools are exempt from property taxes while private businesses are not. In order to compare social rates of return on investments in busi-

[28] The breakdown is as follows:

	1939	*1949*
Noneducational	19.1	21.9
Extension	7.3	5.3
Research	5.6	14.2
Organized activities	5.5	7.1

(See *COEIHE*, Tables 58, 83 and 115.)

[29] See *Statistical Summary of Education, 1939-40,* Vol. II of the *Biennial Survey of Education in the United States, 1938-40,* Washington, 1943, Table 42, footnote 1, p. 44. In 1941-42 it was put at 1.70 (see *Statistical Summary of Education, 1941-42,* Vol. II of the *Biennial Survey of Education in the United States,* Table 38, p. 34).

ness and education, either actual property taxes should be added to the net incomes of businesses or implicit taxes to the cost of education. The implicit annual property tax on educational capital was taken as 1.5 per cent of its value.[30] This amounted to $18 per student in 1939 and $21 in 1949, and was added to other educational costs.

[30] See Blitz, in *Economics of Higher Education*, p. 161.

APPENDIX B

Mathematical Discussion of Relation Between Age, Earnings, and Wealth

1. This appendix derives some relations between the earnings and wealth profiles that were used in section 2 of Chapter VII. If the function $E(j)$ stands for earnings at age j, $r(t,E)$ the instantaneous interest rate at time t and for the earnings function E, wealth at age j would be given by

$$W(j) = \int_{t=j}^{t=\infty} E(t) e^{-\int_{q=j}^{q=t} r(q,E)dq} \, dt. \tag{1}$$

The properties of this very general integral equation are not easily discovered and a number of simplifications are introduced. Interest rates are assumed to be independent of the date or earnings function, so

$$r(t, E) = r. \tag{2}$$

Earnings are assumed to grow at a constant rate for m years and then to equal zero, or

$$E(j) = ae^{bi} \quad 0 \leq j \leq m$$
$$= 0 \quad j > m, \tag{3}$$

where b is the rate of growth.

Time series earnings are often converted into cohort earnings through an expected labor force period that depends on mortality conditions: cohort earnings would equal time series earnings during

Appendix B

this period and zero thereafter. Equation (3) can be so interpreted, with m the expected labor force period, and ae^{bj} earnings during the period. Time series earnings profiles in the United States can be approximated by a simple exponential function, although, as shown in the text, a fuller analysis would certainly have to incorporate a declining rate of growth. The labor force period method of adjusting for mortality, although widely used, is not always accurate and the more appropriate survivorship method is used in the text; the former is, however, a first approximation and its use considerably simplifies the mathematical analysis.

Substituting equations (2) and (3) into (1) gives

$$W(j) = \int_j^m ae^{bt}e^{-r(t-j)}\, dt, \tag{4}$$

and wealth can be explicitly computed as

$$W(j) = \frac{a}{b-r}\left[e^{(b-r)m}e^{rj} - e^{bj}\right], \quad b \neq r \tag{5}$$

$$= a\, e^{rj}\, (m-j), \quad b = r. \tag{5'}$$

Several relations between this wealth function and length of life (m), the rate of growth in earnings (b), and the rate of interest (r) are worked out in the following sections. It is assumed that $b \neq r$, although similar results can easily be proved for $b = r$.

2. The peak wealth age—the age at which wealth is maximized—is positively related to m, b, and r. Differentiating equation (5) yields

$$\frac{\partial W}{\partial j} = \frac{a}{b-r}\left[re^{(b-r)m}e^{rj} - be^{bj}\right], \tag{6}$$

and
$$\frac{\partial^2 W}{\partial j^2} = \frac{a}{b-r}\left[r^2 e^{(b-r)m}e^{rj} - b^2 e^{bj}\right] < 0 \text{ if } \frac{\partial W}{\partial j} = 0.$$

Accordingly, wealth is maximized when

$$re^{(b-r)m}e^{rj} = be^{bj}, \tag{7}$$

and the peak age simply equals

$$\hat{j} = m - \frac{\log b/r}{b-r}. \tag{8}$$

Hence

$$\frac{\partial \hat{j}}{\partial m} = 1 > 0,$$

$$\frac{\partial \hat{j}}{\partial b} = -\frac{1}{(b-r)^2}\left[1 - \left(\frac{r}{b} + \log\frac{b}{r}\right)\right] > 0 \qquad (9)$$

$$\frac{\partial \hat{j}}{\partial r} = -\frac{1}{(b-r)^2}\left[1 - \left(\frac{b}{r} + \log\frac{r}{b}\right)\right] > 0,$$

since

$$1 < \frac{r}{b} + \log\frac{b}{r}, \text{ for all } \frac{b}{r} > 0.$$

A few numerical calculations can illustrate the orders of magnitude involved. If m is taken as 42 years—about the average number spent in the labor force by persons experiencing 1940 mortality rates—r as 8 per cent and b as 3 per cent—roughly the average annual growth in the earnings of 1939 college graduates between ages 30 and 60—$\hat{j}$ would equal 22.4 years, or 40 years if age 18 rather than age 0 were considered the initial year. If b equaled 2.7 per cent—roughly the average growth in earnings of 1939 elementary-school graduates between ages 30 and 60—$\hat{j}$ would equal 20.5 years, or 2 years less than college graduates. If r were 4 per cent, $\hat{j}$ would be 14 and 12 for these college and elementary-school graduates respectively, much lower than when $r =$ .08, but still a difference of 2 years. A reduction of m to 36 years—the average time spent in the labor force after age 18 by nineteenth century slaves—would reduce all peak ages by about 6 years, regardless of the values of b and r.

3. Equations (5) and (6) imply that

$$\frac{\partial W}{\partial j} \bigg/ W = \frac{re^{(b-r)m}e^{ri} - be^{bi}}{e^{(b-r)m}e^{ri} - e^{bi}} \qquad (10)$$

$$= \frac{re^{(b-r)(m-j)} - b}{e^{(b-r)(m-j)} - 1}.$$

Appendix B

By equation (3)

$$\frac{\partial E}{\partial j} \Big/ E = b; \tag{11}$$

so it follows from (10) and (11) that

$$\frac{\partial W}{\partial j} \Big/ W < \frac{\partial E}{\partial j} \Big/ E. \tag{12}$$

Since earnings reach a peak at age m, later than the peak in wealth, equation (12) implies that the ratio of peak to initial values is greater for earnings than wealth.

The rate of change in wealth is positively related to, as well as less than, the rate of change in earnings, or

$$\frac{\frac{\partial W}{\partial j} \Big/ W}{\partial b} > 0. \tag{13}$$

For

$$\frac{\frac{\partial W}{\partial j} \Big/ W}{\partial b} = \frac{-e^{gx} + 1 + gxe^{gx}}{(e^{gx} - 1)^2} > 0, \tag{14}$$

where $x = m - j$ and $g = b - r$, only if

$$e^{gx}(1 - gx) < 1. \tag{15}$$

If $|gx| \geq 1$, eq. (15) clearly holds; if $|gx| < 1$, then

$$\frac{1}{1 - gx} = 1 + gx + (gx)^2 + \cdots, \tag{16}$$

and the infinite series expansion of e^{gx} shows that eq. (15) must hold. Therefore eq. (13) is proven.

Although the rate of change in wealth is greater the greater the rate of change in earnings, the ratio of peak to initial wealth is a smaller fraction of the ratio of earnings at the peak wealth age to initial earnings the greater the rate of increase in earnings. That is,

$$\partial \left[\frac{W(\hat{j})/W(o)}{E(\hat{j})/E(o)} \right] = k < 0. \qquad (17)$$
$$\overline{\qquad\qquad\quad \partial b \qquad\qquad\quad}$$

Since

$$\frac{W(j)}{W(0)} = \frac{e^{(b-r)m}e^{rj} - e^{bj}}{e^{(b-r)m} - 1}, \qquad (18)$$

and

$$\frac{E(j)}{E(0)} = e^{bj}, \qquad (19)$$

$$\frac{W(j)/W(0)}{E(j)/E(0)} = \frac{e^{(b-r)(m-j)} - 1}{e^{(b-r)m} - 1}. \qquad (20)$$

By equation (8)

$$m - \hat{j} = \frac{\log b/r}{b - r},$$

so

$$k = \frac{e^{\log b/r} - 1}{e^{(b/r)m} - 1} = \frac{b/r - 1}{e^{(b-r)m} - 1}. \qquad (21)$$

Hence

$$\frac{\partial k}{\partial b} < 0$$

only if

$$e^{gm} - 1 - gme^{gm} < 0,$$

or only if

$$e^{gm}(1 - gm) < 1. \qquad (22)$$

Equation (22) is simply equation (15) again; therefore (17) has been proven.

4. The equation

$$\frac{\partial W}{\partial x} / W = \frac{ge^{gx}}{e^{gx} - 1} \qquad (23)$$

gives the rate of decline in wealth as the number of remaining years in the labor force (x) declines. Equations (10), (11), and (23) imply that

$$\frac{\partial W}{\partial x} / W + \frac{\partial W}{\partial j} / W = b = \frac{\partial E}{\partial j} / E, \qquad (24)$$

or

$$\frac{\partial W}{\partial x} / W = \frac{\partial E}{\partial j} / E - \frac{\partial W}{\partial j} / W. \qquad (25)$$

Appendix B

The difference between the rates of change in earnings and wealth with respect to age is simply equal to the rate of decline in wealth as the number of remaining years declines.

Equation (23) indicates that wealth declines more rapidly the fewer the years remaining, and declines infinitely fast as these years approach zero. As they go to infinity—life becomes indefinitely long—the rate of decline in wealth approaches $b - r$ if $b > r$, and 0 if $b < r$. Therefore, equations (23) and (24) imply that

$$\lim_{x \to \infty} \frac{\partial W}{\partial j} / W = \min(b, r) \qquad (26)$$

The rate of change in wealth with age approaches the rate of change in earnings only if the latter were less than the discount rate; otherwise the discount rate would be approached, a somewhat surprising result.

5. According to the definition used in the text, the rate of "depreciation" at age j is

$$D(j) = - \frac{\partial W(j)}{\partial j}, \qquad (27)$$

while the rate of "appreciation" is $- D(j) = \frac{\partial W(j)}{\partial j}$. The average rate during the whole period of labor force participation is given by

$$\bar{D} = \frac{1}{m} \int_0^m D(j) \, dj = \frac{-1}{m} \int_0^m \frac{\partial W}{\partial j} \, dj$$

$$= \frac{1}{m} [W(0) - W(m)] = \frac{1}{m} W(0), \qquad (28)$$

since $W(m) = 0$.

Average depreciation divided by average earnings gives the ratio

$$d = \frac{\bar{D}}{\bar{E}} = \frac{\frac{1}{m} W(0)}{\bar{E}} = \frac{\int_0^m E e^{-rj} \, dj}{\int_0^m E \, dj}, \qquad (29)$$

which is the ratio of the present values at the initial age of earnings discounted at the market rate to earnings discounted at a zero rate. This ratio is obviously positively related to the market rate, approaching zero for an infinite, and unity for a zero, rate.

"Permanent" earnings are defined either as

$$E_p(j) = E(j) - D(j),\tag{30}$$

or as

$$E_p(j) = rW(j).\tag{31}$$

so

$$E(j) = D(j) + rW(j),\tag{32}$$

and, therefore, equation (29) can be written as

$$d = \frac{D}{E} = \frac{\dfrac{1}{m}\,W(0)}{r\overline{W} + \dfrac{1}{m}\,W(0)}.\tag{33}$$

Hence d would be smaller the smaller the ratio of initial to average wealth. Section 2 of Chapter VII implies that the latter, in turn, would be smaller the faster the rate of increase in earnings because the rate of increase in wealth is positively related to the rate of increase in earnings.

INDEX

Index